Change Is On The Horizon
by James Rink

Book Production
Copyright © 2012
by
David E. Robinson

Edition, October 2012

Maine-Patriot.com
3 Linnell Circle
Brunswick, Maine 04011

http://maine-patriot.com

Change Is On The Horizon

Change Is On The Horizon
by James Rink

Contents

Change Is On The Horizon

Preface

This book presents James Rink's extraordinary three hour Internet video **"Change is on the Horizon"** in book form. You may want to watch the video before reading this book. Go to **http://tinyurl.com/9xld6u6** for the full version.

After watching **"Change is on the Horizon"** several times, I still found it difficult to retain all of the marvelous details and facts packed within this educational documentary.

So James has permitted me to publish this video in book form so that I can use it as a reverence book, by highlighting the many important outstanding facts it reveals, without having to watch it all the way through, each time, to find what I need.

"Change is on the Horizon" is the epic story of how the world lost its soul, and how it will gain it back, directed and narrated by James Rink. This project took James Rink three years and thousands of hours of editing and reediting to complete it.

Part 1 - **Dawn of the Golden Age** - discusses how Saint Germain helped to bring about the beginnings of an enlightened era which soon fell into darkness under the realms of the Illuminati and a corrupted Masonic order.

Part 2 - **The American Federal Empire** - shows that America was always meant to be a shinning beacon of prosperity and freedom to the world. But the machinations of British bankers and the Rothschild dynasty soon destroyed all that was once good in this great land.

Part 3 - **The Farmers Claim Program** - Discusses how a class action lawsuit, brought about in the early 1990's, led to the creation of **NESARA**, the **National Economic Security and Reformation Act**, which will ultimately tear the New World Order apart, and the international bankers' plans from under their feet.

David E. Robinson
Brunswick, Maine
Book and Cover Design

~   ~   ~   ~   ~   ~

"SIC FULGET IN UMBRAS"
"TRUTH IS ENVELOPED IN OBSCURITY"

Change Is On The Horizon

Introduction
June 18, 2010

Since the fall of Atlantis, Satan and his minions have been working tirelessly to end all goodness on this planet. But God and the brotherhood of light had put together their own plan to defeat the dark side. Throughout history many prophets have come forth to speak of the coming of a golden age of humanity. This truth was made known only to fall silent on the deaf ears of the ignorant masses. But **change is on the horizon.**

By the time of the renaissance, humanity had begun to rise from its slumber. Slowly mysticism and superstition began to be replaced with science and logic. It is here, 400 years ago, at the height of Tudor England, where this story begins.

Change Is On The Horizon

PART I
The Dawn of the Golden Age

A secret marriage was arranged between Queen Elizabeth the 1st (1533-1603) and Sir Robert Dudley (1533-1588). Due to Dudley's political ambitions the queen chose to maintain her virgin queen status. From this marriage came forth Francis Bacon (1561-1626) who was raised by an adopted family. At the age of 15, while his parents were arguing, he over heard the truth, that he was the future heir of the King of England. All his life the queen kept dangling in front of him the mantle of power.

To be or not to be, that was his question. Alas, it was not to be, In 1603 Queen Elizabeth appointed King James VI (1566-1625) of Scotland to be her successor. Instead of letting this defeat him, Francis chose to rise above his circumstances in the pursuit of scholarly and political interests. He had the King James Bible translated. He wrote the Shakespearean sonnets. He persuaded King James I to charter Newfoundland and was an officer in the Virginia Company. He was King James's Lord Chancellor. And he fathered deductive reasoning, which set the grounds for science and technology to liberate humanity.

Secretly he was a master of the alchemical sciences and the occult. It was here that he began to remember his past lives, as the Prophet Samuel, Plato, Saint Joseph, Merlin, Roger Bacon, and Christopher Columbus.

When he was the prophet Samuel, he helped liberate the children of Abraham from the bondage of corrupt priests and the Philistines. In the 5th century while Europe was falling into the Dark Ages, he returned again as Merlin, to help King Arthur establish Britain into a stronghold against ignorance and superstition. A place where Christ's achievements could flower, and devotion to the one Source could prosper in the quest for the Holy Grail. It was later in the nineteenth century when his efforts blossomed, when the United Kingdom became a place where industry and individual initiative could thrive as never before, in 12,000 years.

As the medieval alchemist Roger Bacon (1214-1294) he predicted the invention of a hot-air balloon, a flying machine, a magnifying glass, and mechanically propelled ships and carriages. And amazingly, he wrote of them as if he had actually seen them!

He believed "True knowledge stems not from the authority of others, nor from a blind allegiance to antiquated dogmas, but instead is a highly personal experience — a light that is communicated only to the innermost privacy of the individual through the impartial channels of all knowledge and of all thought." Because of the heretical nature of these beliefs, the church imprisoned him where he remained for his final years.

In his "Opus Majus" he wrote of a voyage of three ships and the discovery of a New World.

"The sea between the end of Spain on the west and the beginning of India on the east is navigable in a very few days if the wind is favorable."

In his next life as Christopher Columbus he was inspired by these words and along with a prophecy made by Isaiah, he knew a New World would be found whereby God would:

"Recover the remnant of his people...and shall assemble the outcasts of Israel, and gather together the dispersed of Judah from the four corners of the earth." — Isaiah 11:12.

When Francis Bacon became conscious of these incarnations, he sought those hidden treasures he placed away until his rebirth.

At the age of 12, Francis conceived of a time when mankind would go through a period of great restoration. In 1620 he placed this vision for humanity in his book "The Great Instauration" in which he formulized how to change "The whole wide world," through the restoration of true knowledge after centuries of obscurity and neglect. It was here, that he first devised the scientific method that ultimately launched a new English Renaissance.

Many of his ideas were kept in the shroud of secret societies, in order to hide from the prying eyes of church officials. With help from his brother Anthony, and some friends who were students at Gray's Inn Law School, they created a secret society known as the "The Knights of the Helmet." They chose this name from the Goddess Athena who is depicted as wearing Pallas's helmet of invisibility and carrying a golden spear of knowledge. The Goddess Athena brings about wisdom, intellect, and the moral side of human life.

Athena's helmet of invisibility represents her silent war against ignorance and sloth. The Knights of the Helmet also considered themselves invisible warriors against ignorance and sloth, as they secretly worked to expand the English language by creating new literatures, not written in Latin, but instead in words all Englishmen could understand such as found within the King James Bible.

In 1611 the King James edition of the bible was commissioned in order to unite the Anglican and Puritan church leaders. After a long series of edits by nondescript translators, the final draft was handed to King James, who then passed it on to Francis Bacon so that he could revise the bible into a marvelous piece of literary work which is still being used today.

Many of these works were written anonymously under pen names such as William Shakespeare. Francis chose this name because the goddess Athena was known to carry a golden spear of knowledge, which she would use to strike at the serpent of ignorance. When sunlight would strike her spear it was known to tremble thus the people would say she was shaking her spear again, hence the word "Shakespeare". In a symbolic gesture Francis would shake his pen, as a spear of knowledge to slay the dragons of foolishness.

Written within the Shakespearean plays is a hidden cipher which shows Francis Bacon not only as the true heir of the King of England but also of Queen Elizabeth's secret marriage to the Earl of Leicester and her proceeding two sons.

For upon his birth Francis Bacon was given over to Sir Nicholas and Lady Anne who pleaded with the queen for the life of the child. Queen Elizabeth rejected her son because she feared her subjects would choose a male heir over herself to rule the kingdom. Some historical documents hint of this secret marriage and her two children such as found within this portrait*, however any talk of this during the time of Queen Elizabeth would have resulted in imprisonment or death.

*Isaac de Larrey

After a happy childhood spent with Sir Nicholas and Lady Anne, on his 12th birthday, he was enrolled in Cambridge University. Mysteriously, Queen Elizabeth provided the funds for his education. At the age of 15, he discovered the true identity of his royal blood, so Queen Elizabeth sent Francis aboard, to France, placing him at a comfortable distance from her throne.

While in France he studied cipher codes to learn new ways to protect confidential information in England, and he also worked with Masonic secret societies which sought to reform the French language. Three years later, upon his return to England, he brought back these same ideas and created a secret society known as the Knights of the Helmet which through their literary works, would ultimately modernize the English language by standardizing the spelling of words.

The Knights of the Helmet was part of a larger movement of secret societies found within Rosicrucian teachings which dated back to the time of Atlantis. The Rosicrucian's were a loose knit group of secret societies which believed knowledge or wisdom was eternal and should be freely available to those who seek it.

Just like with the Knights of the Helmet, the Rosicrosse secret society was also part of this movement. The Rosicrosse is shorthand for the 'The Society of the Golden and Rosy Cross' which was founded in 1571 to protect Queen Elizabeth after she was excommunicated by the pope and secretly they sought to bring about "universal enlightenment through the use of the alchemical process."

The golden cross symbolized the transmutation of the base elements into spiritual light. The Red Cross symbolized the heraldic color of the metal gold. These colors were often associated with Saint George and Archangel Michael. And the Rose symbolized the heart of the cross where one can find love, intelligence, and enlightenment within the human soul. Just like with Athena's helmet of invisibility, members of the Rosicrosse would make silent oaths under the principle of "sub-rosa" or beneath the rose. They believed it was best to be discreet and conceal some things while revealing others in order to create a treasure trail to those who seek truth.

And as Athena would shake her spear at the snakes of ignorance so could Saint George shake his spear at the dragons of vice. Members of these societies understood that if an individual could be a powerful force of change, so could they in larger numbers slay the dragons of the world.

It was here, as a member of the Rosicrosse secret society, that Francis Bacon became inspired to write his famous "Great Instauration" which would restore paradise on earth through knowledge and virtue.

In addition to the Rosicrosse and the Knight's of the Helmet secret societies, was the Freemason secret society, whose members passed down the secrets of building the massive cathedrals and castles of Europe.

After the death of Queen Elizabeth in 1603, King James succeeded to the throne. During his reign, Francis was promoted to Viscount St. Albans and Lord Chancellor, which was the highest position of power one could obtain in that era, other than the king himself.

He was given the task to reform freemasonry, which in late Elizabethan England was more of a social clique for the elite. He sought to change *operative* freemasonry of the medieval stone guilds, into *speculative* freemasonry, that is, a fraternal order of philosophers that would recreate the world as God made it, and not as men or the church made it, a place where religious and political strife could be placed aside under its three great Masonic principles of brotherly love, relief for the poor, and seekers of truth.

He then redrafted the Nine Degrees of the Knight's of Templar into thirty three degrees which became the basis of modern day freemasonry. Many of these initiations were based on Christian ethics with a focus on the realization of one's own *inner Christ consciousness.*

Francis chose 33 initiations of freemasonry from a simple Elizabethan cipher which equaled to the numerical value of his signature. By assigning a number for each letter of the alphabet, the name Bacon equals to 33.

B A C O N
(B=2, A=1, C=3, 0=14, N =13)
2 +1+ 3+ 14+ 13 = 33

Continuing his mission that he first began as Christopher Columbus, he persuaded King James to sign the Virginia Charter, which began the colonization of the New World with England's first permanent colony at Jamestown.

Here his Masonic teachings of inner divine potential, freedom, and enlightenment spread, which later resulted in the creation of the United States of America under its Masonic founding fathers.

In his book "The New Atlantis" he foretold of a pacific island where science prevailed over ignorance and superstition. This island had no ruler's but instead a learned council of men who had proven themselves through scientific achievement. He envisioned the New World, as this New Atlantis; a place where freedom and peace would reign under a Masonic order without despotic rulers trying to control their fellow man; a place where the heritage of the House of Solomon could once again prosper under a golden age culture of science and logic.

By 1620, his literary fame and political success had begun to spread, which created much jealously amongst his fellow members of parliament. Eventually they accused him of corruption which was later proven unjust. After falling from public grace he continued his work, secretly reforming the Rosicrucian Mystery schools and Masonic fraternities. His motto of *"One lives best by the hidden life"* describes him perfectly, as his efforts continue to secretly influence humanity.

Francis once said "The great end of life is not knowledge but action." True to his word, in 1626 he faked his own "Philosophers death" and attended his funeral in disguise with another body in the coffin. He then traveled to the Rákóczi (*Ra-coat-see*) Mansion in the Carpathian Mountain region of Transylvania, which is now located in modern day Romania.

Here during the reign of Ferenc (*F(e)-re-nc*) Rákóczi the 1st (1645-1676), he continued his studies of alchemy preparing him for his physical Ascension under the watchful eye of Master R, who was the Great Divine Director.

After making two million right decisions spanning hundreds of thousands of years of incarnations he was granted ascension. The highest form of alchemy is not the transmutation of the base elements into gold but instead the transmutation of the soul into oneness with the Creator. On May 1, 1684, he finally mastered these secrets and ascended into the 14th dimension, transmuting his mortal body into an immortal angel conquering death itself.

After the ascension process occurs, normally a soul would choose to move on to serve in higher dimensions. However, Francis requested to join the Great White Brotherhood of Light, who are souls that have vowed to stick with the earth, until the day all humanity could ascend. These so called ascended masters rarely interact with humanity. But Francis chose a different path; he wanted to return back in a human body to teach others how to overcome the laws of the physical universe and to help usher in the coming golden age of humanity.

His karmic board granted his request and he materialized a new body as the Comte de Saint Germain (*Kont-da-sain-ger-mon*) or the Count of Saint Germain. He chose his name from the Latin word, Sanctus Germanus, meaning 'Holy Brother'.

The Count was known as the "Wonderman of Europe" as he would amaze nobility and royalty alike, many of which commented on his elaborate shoes studded with $40,000 dollar diamonds and pearls. Amazingly, he was able to turn rocks into diamonds and remove any flaws. He could write two poems with both hands at the same time, he could read a book by waving his hand over it; he spoke every language, traveled by thought, and worked for peace.

He was an accomplished pianist, singer, and violinist. Those who have known him said he played the violin equal to or even surpassing the greatest virtuosos of that period, and Saint Germain even remarked that he had reached the extreme limit possible for his talent. He was also known for his artwork and alchemy. He taught Franz Mesmer his fundamental ideas on personal magnetism and hypnosis, and he initiated Cagliostro (*Cal-ee-os-tro*) into the Masonic order.

And with his "elixir of life" and positive thinking he never aged at all. According to Germain, "It is the activity of our nerves, the flame of our desire, the acid of our fears, which daily consume our organism. He who succeeds in raising himself above his emotions, in suppressing in himself anger and the fear of illness, is capable of overcoming the attrition of the years and attaining an age at least double that at which men now die of old age."

He served as a counselor to kings and princes; he fought against deceptive ministers, and he handed the torch of wisdom to Masons and Rosicrucian's alike. Prince Karl von Hesse described him as "one of the greatest philosophers who ever lived, the friend of humanity, whose heart was concerned only with the happiness of others."

He worked closely with royalty to help usher in a United States of Europe. But these plans came to an end when Napoleon sought power for his own demise. Despite this failure, he was instrumental in the creation of the United States of America, which he knew would usher in a golden age which would last forever.

After Saint Germain ascended, he remained in Transylvania, but details of this period of his life remain cloaked in the shroud of mystery. Historians hint that he was possibly adopted into the royal house of Hungary as the third son of Francis Racozy the second, using a different name and identity as a convenient disguise.

By the year 1700, Transylvania was the conquered territory of the Austro-Hungarian Empire. When Francis Rakoczi the second (1676-1735) became aware of how Austrian Emperor Leopold, had placed his subjects under the bondage of high taxes and oppressive government; he led a successful revolt to liberate his people. But it is unclear what role if any Saint Germain played in this plot.

Rumors of an elixir of life which prolonged his lifespan followed Germain throughout his years. In 1710 Saint Germain appeared in Venice where he met the musician Jean-Philippe Rameau (*Zhan feeleep–ra-muo*) and the ambassadress to Vienna, the (*Co-n-tes duh jon-lee*) Comtesse de Genlis. He introduced himself under the name of (*Mar-kee-duh-mon-fai-ra*) Marquis de Montferrat (*Markee duh mon* (nasal again) *faira* (t is silent). At that time, he appeared to be 40 years old, and gave the countess a memorable gift of this magical elixir, that maintained her youth for a very long time.

50 years later, Comtesse de Georgy (*Co n tes duh jon-lee*) met him once, while visiting Madame de Pompadour's house, who was the mistress of King Louis XV. She inquired if his father had been in Venice back in 1710. The Count replied. "No, Madame, but I myself was living in Venice at the end of the last, and the beginning of this century. I had the honor to pay your court then, and you were kind enough to admire a little Barcarolle (*Bar·ca·role*) of my composing." The countess could not believe it. "But if that is true," she gasped, "you must be at least a hundred years old!" The Count smiled. "That, Madame, is not impossible!"

Suspecting the Count was being less than truthful Madam de Pompadour inquired again about the countess and her tale of a so called elixir of life. Germain replied with a smile. "It is not impossible; but I confess it is likely that this lady, for whom I have the greatest respect, is talking nonsense." Undaunted, Madame Pompadour tried many times to get that elixir, but Germain would not share his secrets, however he was able to make her a cosmetic which enhanced her beauty.

Hints of his true age continued to surround him with intrigue when in 1723, Saint Germain showed the mother of Comtesse de Genlis (*Con tes duh jon-lee*), a miniature portrait of his own mother which he kept on his arm. When she saw a beautiful woman dressed in a costume unfamiliar to her own time. The countess inquired, "To what period does this costume belong?" The Count merely smiled and changed the subject.

If Saint Germain truly had an elixir of life, it would mean he had ultimately mastered the secrets of the philosophers' stone, which medieval alchemist's believed could transmute the base metals such as lead, into gold. It seemed likely if anyone could have figured this out it would have been Saint Germain as he closely worked with the Fratres Lucis (*Frahters loo-sis*) "Brothers of Light", and with the "Knights and Brothers of Asia" who studied the Rosicrucian and Hermetic sciences of alchemy of which the three parts of the Azoth constituted the "philosopher's stone".

No one really knows if Saint Germain was truly able to turn lead into gold, but in 1727 it appears he had done just that. These secret money making techniques were shared with certain German bankers and monarchies in the hopes that the wealth generated would benefit all humanity, but instead they squandered it for themselves.

So in 1729, he abandoned support of these power brokers, and created the **"World Trust"**. From its inception he stipulated that the World Trust would be released by the year 2000. But this is not an easy task to do, as you will soon see. Saint Germain realized that humanity would never be ready for the knowledge and technology of the Aquarian age, until mankind could put aside their destructive sciences and religions, and accept the heart of which lies of both, that is, *to enter one's heart,* and harness one's own unlimited potential.

After the establishment of the World Trust, Saint Germain traveled to the court of the Shah of Persia, where he remained from 1737 to 1742. Here he studied the secrets of nature, of which he learned the closely-guarded science of precipitating and enlarging gemstones, which was manifested through psychic powers. The Counts love affair with precious stones was well known among his friends and associates.

At one point, Saint Germain showed a small box to Madame du Pompadour, which contained topazes, emeralds, and diamonds, worth at least $90 million dollars in today's money. While in Paris the aristocracy marveled at his diamond encrusted shoe buckles, but yet no one could identity him or his great source of wealth.

Many years later, Madame du Hausset (madam dyoo osay), described within in her memoirs, how Saint Germain wore an assortment of diamond rings of great value and how his watch and snuff box were ornamented with a profusion of precious stones. She also had witnessed Saint Germain remove a flaw from a large diamond which had belonged to King Louis XV, increasing its value from 6,000 livres to 10,000 livres. The King was never able to get over this astonishment and would often confide that if Saint Germain could increase the value of gemstones, he must be a millionaire.

Yet no one could discover his source of wealth as he never kept any records or held any traceable bank accounts. He would always stay in fine hotels and apartments; and would always have as much cash available as he needed. When a curious minister spent two years keeping tabs on him, he concluded that Saint Germain paid for everything in real money, but did not have a source of a financial backing. When Saint Germain was confronted about this he responded. "I hold the whole of nature in my hands, and as God created the world, I can draw what I want out of nothing."

In 1743 he traveled to London where for two years he remained in a home on St. Martin's Street. During this time he conducted many alchemical experiments within his laboratory, probably manufacturing artificial diamonds.

He was known to frequently visit the Kit-Kat Club where he would mingle with members of the highest nobility. He astounded members with two inventions he was working on, the steam train and steam boat, both of which were predicted by Roger Bacon. Twenty years later James Watt prototyped his idea by building a steam engine, and later in 1829, George Stephenson built the first public railway operated by a steam train.

After his stay in London he visited his friend Frederick the Great in his castle of Sans-Souci (*Son-soo-see*) in Potsdam where Voltaire was also an honored guest. In a letter addressed to Fredrick, Voltaire later wrote, "The Comte de Saint Germain is a man who was never born, who will never die, and who knows everything."

In 1749 while at Versailles, King Louis XV was introduced to the Count by his Peer of France, to relieve some of his boredom. Soon after, he meets the King's Mistress, Madame Pompadour, and becomes a court favorite. The king was captivated by his stories of travel all around the world and his wisdom of the alchemical arts. In a gesture of good faith, Saint Germain gave away his invention of inexpensive dyes, which helped increase the employment and wealth of the Nation while lowering the manufacturing cost of clothing so that commoners could dress as good as the nobility class.

In 1755 King Louis XV recruited him to travel to Southeast Asia to infiltrate the British East India Company as a spy. He journeyed in the same ship as General Robert Clive, possibly as the ship's doctor. Here, he became aware of the British schemes to subjugate India at the Battle of Plassey (*Pa-lass-ie*) and the recapture of Calcutta. Thanks to his efforts, he saved the lives of many French troops who were protecting the Indian people at that time.

When he returned to Europe in 1758, King Louis XV granted him a royal favor for his work in India, with a suite of rooms at the Royal Chateau of Chambord, in Touraine, to continue his experiments of alchemy that King Louis XV sometimes participated in. In a letter written in 1773, Graf Karl Cobenzl (*Coh-ben-zle*) of Brussels commented about these alchemical experiments, "of which the most important were the transmutation of iron into a metal as beautiful as gold".

In 1762 he traveled to Russia in a secret plot which put Catherine the Great on the throne. Then in 1774 he returned back to France to deliver a message to the now crowned King Louis the XVI and Marie Antoinette. Saint Germain delivered a warning of an approaching conspiracy that would soon occur within the next 15 years, which would create "a blood-thirsty republic, whose scepter will be the executioner's knife." Sadly, this warning went unheeded, and among the final entries within Marie Antoinette's dairy, she recorded her regret at ignoring the Count's advice.

Between 1774 and 1784 the Count spent his time traveling throughout Germany and Austria petitioning the monarchies to work together to avert the French Revolution and to create a United States of Europe. Though the monarchies enjoyed being entertained by Saint Germain's marvelous alchemical experiments; neither they nor their jealous ministers, wished to relinquish their power to a unified Europe.

With his plans in Europe crumbling apart he then turned his eyes to the now prosperous new world, because he knew America would play a key role in raising people's consciousness into the golden age.

On a steamy July 4th, 1776, the most influential leaders of the American colonies were locked in Independence Hall debating whether they should risk a traitor's death by signing the Declaration of Independence. Even though the doors were locked, Saint Germain appeared in the balcony and delivered a fiery speech calling forth the founding fathers to "Sign that document!"

He continued, "The words of the Declaration will live in the world long after our bones are dust. To the mechanic they will speak hope, to the slave in the mines, freedom, but to the coward kings these words will speak tones of warning they cannot choose but hear. Sign that parchment! Sign!"

"If the next moment the gibbet's rope is about your neck! Sign! By all hopes in life and death, as men, as husbands, as fathers, brothers, or be accursed for forever. Sign! Not only for yourselves but for all ages, for that parchment will be the textbook of freedom, the bible of the rights of man forever. I would beg you to sign that parchment for the sake of those millions whose very breath is now hushed in intense expectation as they look up to you for the awful words: 'You are Free.'"

Unafraid of the repercussions by King George the Third, these brave men boldly rushed forward and signed their names. So inspired by this speech, John Hancock signed his name in large bold letters so that the King would be able to read it without his spectacles.

During the Revolutionary War Saint Germain was also instrumental in persuading King Louis XVI to appoint the French General Rochambeau (*Roe shim boe*) over 6,000 troops, to serve in George Washington's Continental Army. Historians now agree that this assistance played a critical role in a decisive victory for the American forces.

The signing of the Declaration of Independence eventually led the way to the liberation of the American Colonies into a more perfect union, a place where the virtues of righteousness and freedom could reign under the banner of the United States of America.

But trouble was now brewing in Europe. Not only were his plans for a United States of Europe crumbling apart so too was his Masonic secret society which had now been infiltrated by the Satanic faction of Bavarian Lodge of Freemasonry. Who under the helm of a Jewish Rothschild agent, Adam Weishaupt (*Adam wise-hoff*), began to rewrite Masonic initiations based on Luciferic teachings of the Talmud in which enlightenment would be attain through worship of Lucifer as the ultimate light bearer.

They now dubbed themselves the Illuminati and sought to divide the "goyim", or the non-Jews through political, social, economic, or religious means. The Rothschild's planned to use the Illuminati and freemasonry to destroy the masses so that they could take over the world, and steal all the people's gold, so it could be returned to King Solomon's temple in Jerusalem. This is why the Rothschild's financed the creation of Israel and why they are considered its patron saint.

This was in direct opposition to Saint Germain's version of freemasonry, in which he envisioned universal enlightenment of one's own inner divine potential would spread to a small group of initiates and then in turn to other initiates in a vast spiral of spiritual radiation to all humanity.

But much to Saint Germain's horror; these dark teachings began to spread like a blight within the Masonic lodges. To counteract the Illuminati movement, he recruited a close group of friends, including Prince Charles of Hesse-Kassel (*Hes-cas-el*) and Cagliostro (*Cal-ee-os-tro*), to create a secret society known as the Philalethes (*Fill-a-LAY-thess*), which taught that mankind had infinite possibilities and that they must strive to release themselves of physical matter in order to communicate with higher intelligences.

But the Philalethes (*Fill-a-LAY-thess*) society never caught on. At the 1782 Wilhelmsbad (*Wil-helms-bad*) Convention, the lodges voted to merge freemasonry with the Illuminati, thus creating the notorious form of modern day freemasonry. Three years later, at the great Paris Convention of 1785 he, and along with Cagliostro, Franz Mesmer, and Saint Martin tried in vain, to bring reconciliation amongst the Rosicrucian's, illuminatist, and mason's alike. Had Saint Germain been successful in redirecting freemasonry into a philosopher's organization, such as the Philalethes (*Fill-a-LAY-thess*), he would have been able to avert the evil chain of events which have since occurred in preceding generations.

After the convention of 1785, Saint Germain fell into disgrace, this time the Jesuits had falsely accused him of immorality, conspiracy to create anarchy, and infidelity.

As a result, he played an increasingly diminished role within the very society he had founded nearly 200 years prior.

Soon after 1785, the Masonic lodges began to systemically erase all traces of Saint Germain from their order. But with one blazing exception, the letter 'G' which symbolizes the word Germain, can still be found between the Masonic square and compass. Despite freemasonry's attempts to erase all traces of Saint Germain from their order, his vision presses on; humanity will be set free from its shackles of slavery and death.

After the Masonic schism, Saint Germain worked with his close friend Prince Charles of Hesse-Kassel in Schleswig (*Shles-wig*), Germany, where they would conduct experiments in alchemy. Growing weary of his failed efforts in Europe, Saint Germain sought to remove attention from himself in a more private life. So on February 27, 1784, Saint Germain once again faked his own death.

After his funeral, the behavior of Prince Charles became uncommunicative and he would often change the subject if anyone spoke of the Count. Those who knew the Prince closely became convinced that not only was the Count still alive but it appeared the Prince was an accomplice to Saint Germain's pretended death.

Most historians believe the Count had now died at this point, however he resurfaced once again in order to block the attempts of the illuminati from toppling the French monarchy. In the 18th century the Rothschild family had managed to become fabulously wealthy by loaning money to the monarchies, but now they desired to open up new markets. They wanted to capture the other 97% of the population who were not royalty, to create a new class of consumers which could then be enslaved with debt. So they recruited Adam Weishaupt to provide Maximilien Robespierre with their plans for a French Revolution.

Early one Sunday morning in 1788 Saint Germain visited the (*Con-tes-da-day-mar*) Comtesse d'Adhémar, who was one of Marie-Antoinette's ladies-in-waiting. He requested an audience with the Queen to discuss ways to advert the French Revolution. When she arrived, the Count told her, "Madame, for twenty years I was on intimate terms with the late King, who deigned to listen to me with kindness. He made use of my poor abilities on several occasions, and I do not think he regretted giving me his confidence."

The Count then informed her of a plot by the Encyclopaedists and the Duke de Chartres (*Duc duh shar-truh*) to overthrow the monarchy. He instructed her to inform the king of this coming conspiracy, and requested that the king would not consult with his Chief Advisor, the Comte de Maurepas (*Cont duh morpa*).

But the king ignored his warning and immediately consulted with the Count. And in the midst of the conversation Saint Germain appeared to confront the Comte de Maurepas with his plans to commit treachery and said to him. "In opposing yourself to my seeing the monarch, you are losing the monarchy, for I have but a limited time to give to France. This time over, I shall not be seen here again, until after three successive generations have gone down to the grave."

The second warning from Saint Germain came on July 14, 1789, after the Queen said farewell to the (*Du-shes-*

duh-pole-en-yac) Duchesse de Polignac (du (the hard to pronounce u) shes duh pole-en-yac), she opened a letter and read: "My words have fallen on your ears in vain, and you have reached the period of which I informed you. All the Polignacs (*Pole-en-yacs*) and their friends are doomed to death. The Comte d'Artois (*Cont dar-twa*) will perish."

On October 5, 1789, Comtesse d'Adhémar (*Con-tes da-day-mar*) received Saint Germain's farewell letter, in which he wrote. "All is lost, Countess! This sun is the last which will set on the monarchy; tomorrow it will exist no more. My advice has been scorned. Now it is too late. . ." He then asked the Countess to meet him early the next morning.

At which, she was informed that the time when he could help France had now past. He continued, "I can do nothing now. My hands are tied by one stronger than myself. The hour of repose is past, and the decrees of Providence must be fulfilled." He then foretold of the death of the Queen, the complete ruin of the House of Bourbon, and the rise of Napoleon."

One Hundred years after his ascension, Saint Germain had brought much enlightenment to the royal courts of Europe, and thanks to his efforts, the creation of the United States of America. Because of this service to humanity, the Great White Brotherhood of Light granted him the office of the Chohan (*Show-han*) of the Seventh Ray.

According to occult philosophy, the Seven Rays are seven metaphysical principles that govern both individuals, and 2,158 year Astrological cycles. Our current astrological **Age of Pisces** is dominated by religion and superstitions, soon this will be replaced with the **Age of Aquarius** which will bring about knowledge and wisdom. As director of the Chohan (*Show-han*) of the Seventh Ray, Saint Germain is responsible for transmuting the old energies of the past, in order to bring about the **Christ consciousness** of coming, golden age of Aquarius. This is why Saint Germain is sometimes referred to as the "The Cosmic Master of the Age of Aquarius".

After he became a cosmic master, Saint Germain was not permitted to work with any more individuals, with the exception of Napoleon, whom he backed and trained. But when Napoleon misused his power, for his own demise, Saint Germain withdrew his support.

At the end of the 18th century, his efforts to unify Europe now lied in ruins. While the Rothschild's continued to engulf the masses in their costly wars, the satanic cult of the illuminati was now rotting out all of the Masonic lodges. There was little else he could do but wait for a better time in which humanity would be more receptive to the ideas of a golden age. So he took a break from European politics and settled in Tibet. In 1790 Saint Germain confided his future plans with his Austrian friend Franz Grae-ffer, saying:

"Tomorrow night I am off. I am much needed in Constantinople, then in England, there to prepare two new inventions which you will have in the next century — trains and steamboats. Toward the end of this century, I shall disappear out of Europe, and betake myself to the region of the Himalayas. I will rest; I must rest. Exactly in 85 years will people again set eyes on me. . . Farewell."

While in Tibet, Saint Germain studied under the Trans-Himalayan Brotherhood as a Shaberon (*Shab-pe-lon*)

Master; who are exalted teachers known to possess wonderful powers. Little else is known of this period, but it's likely he could have traveled into the inner earth tunnels of Shambhala, to study with other ascended masters.

True to his promise, 85 years later, Saint Germain returned to Europe with a new goal in mind. In 1875, Saint Germain convinced the royal families and nations under colonial rule to merge their assets into one account known as the **Combined International Collateral Accounts** of the **Global Debt Facility**. They agreed to do this because they wanted to wait for the right time to release these funds so that it could benefit all the worlds' people. Only Kings or Queens, Presidents, Prime Ministers, and in some cases Minster's of Finance are granted access to these accounts.

The **collateral accounts** contain a minimum of 20 million metric tons of Gold, thousands of tons of Platinum and Silver, and thousands of boxes of precious gems, Sovereign Certificates which are collateralized by other mineral wealth including, Oil, Copper, Uranium, and Nickel. Plus, there are also works of art, sovereign monarchian treasures, and ancient treasures including Aztec, Egyptian, and King Solomon's gold.

Saint Germain placed the collateral accounts within the newly created "Foundation Divine" which also contains the "World Trust", created back in 1729. After 250 years of compound interest the World Trust has now mushroomed into a net worth in excess of **one quattuordecillion dollars**, or a 1, with 45 zeros!

$1,000,000,000,000,000,000,000,000,000,000,000,000,000,000,000.

Enough money to buy a gold cube the size of the orbit of Saturn, so astronomical most people will not believe it!

These figures may appear to be far-fetched, considering the world GDP is $55 trillion dollars annually. However, governments maintain two sets of accounting books, one which is displayed to the public, which contains "official" data issued by the government, and another secretive version which is used between sovereign entities. It is this secretive ledger which contains both the **Collateral Accounts** and Saint Germain's **World Trust**. Some of this wealth is stored in different dimensions, but much of it is stored under **international treaty custodianship rules** within the world's major banking houses. In the case of the collateral accounts they are held within the **Institutional Parent Administration Account of the Federal Reserve** under the control of the Bank of International Settlements and in turn, the Foundation Divine.

This wealth is intended to be used to buy out all illuminati controlled governments, oil corporations, media conglomerates, banking houses, pharmaceutical cartels, and it would zero out all debt. It estimated it would cost a minimum of $100 quintillion dollars just to correct the world's current economic problems. In order for these funds to reach the common man it must travel down through a series of 30,000 different trust funds beginning with the World Trust.

LEVEL ONE

The top level contains the World Trust and remains under the trusteeship of Master Saint Germain. Under his orders the World Court will activate the funding process.

LEVEL TWO

Level two contains 180 royal trusts which are under the control of the trustees in various sovereign countries. Examples include the French Trust, the Russian Trust, and the Vatican Trust.

LEVEL THREE

Level three are the various illuminati family trusts which are under the control of the trustees of the world's wealthiest families including the Warburg Trust, the Rothschild Trust, and the Rockefeller Trust.

LEVEL FOUR

Level four contains the 250 plus Corporate Trusts under the control of the trustees from the world's most powerful companies and corporations, including General Electric, Lockheed, and AT&T.

LEVEL FIVE

Level five contains the wealth from enlighten robber baron children which was placed aside to be used for the benefit of all humanity; these are known as the **Prosperity Program Trusts** and **Bank Roll Programs**, and they are managed by the IMF, under the guidance of Saint Germain. All together there are 72 various bank roll programs, including Bergavine, Omega, and Freedom. The largest trust fund is Freedom, and this must be funded first; when this happens Saint Germain's wealth will finally reach the hands of all humanity.

But if a problem occurs in this chain, the funding window will close. As the funds travel through each level they must be signed off by the 4 to 5 trustees per trust, if the trustees decide to block the money, then the funding process comes to an end.

With each trust level, the trustee must use only certain designated "safe" banks and sign the proper documents with only certain designated banking personnel at those banks. Should this process be activated and then stalled by deceitful bankers or trustees, or if the deadline for funding certain trusts is not met in a timely manner, then the funding window will close. But this is the problem; members of the Bush and Clinton families have been blocking the release of these funds, because they are overseeing many of the trusts as trustees.

After World War II, from 1945 to 1995, the assets in the Collateral Accounts were managed by **The Trillenium Trilateral** (*Try-part-tite*) **Tripartite Commission** representing the United States of America, the United Kingdom, and France. This commission selected the dollar as an international reserve currency and gave the CIA legal responsibility to protect the collateral assets. Nations which did not want a permanent CIA presence on their soil would be allowed to subcontract the protection under the same terms and conditions of the treaties. Extensions of this agreement were expanded through **international treaties**, some of which are still classified as top secret.

> *Jekyll Island Treaty (1910)*
> *The London Treaty (1920)*
> *The Second Plan of the Experts (1929)*
> *The Hague Agreement (1930)*

The Far East Combined Depositories Agreement (1932 – 1945)
The Bretton Woods Agreement (1944)
The B.I.S. / Allies Agreement (1948)
The Green Hilton Agreement (1963)
The Schweitzer Conventions (1968)
The Election / Appointment of Sole Arbiter Agreements (1995)
The Washington Panel (1998)
The Treaty for Respecting the Rights (2003)

With the CIA now in charge of protecting these assets it didn't take long before problems arrived. Sadly, certain rouge elements within the CIA and the bush family have managed to steal over $200 trillion dollars from the collateral accounts stored in places like the Philippines, Thailand, and Russia.

In 1981, Ronald Regan commissioned Leo Wanta to steal $27 and a half trillion dollars from the collateral accounts in Russia, which was then used to crash the ruble, collapsing the Soviet Union. This money belongs to the Russian people and must be returned back to them.

In the 1980's, while V.K. Durham was flipping through an old bible, she found an 1875 Peruvian Gold Certificate with a face value of $1000 dollars plus accrued interest. Today this bond is worth over $6.5 trillion dollars, collateralized by gold from within the collateral accounts. When George bush Senior learned of this gold certificate he tried unsuccessfully to get his hands on it. Eventually V.K. Durham lost control over the money, and now it sits within Saint Germain's World Trust.

Instead of hiding this wealth somewhere in the United States, like Fort Knox, they chose to stash this loot for their own personal benefit, in all places . . . a CIA controlled depository in (*Mon-ta-ve-da-oo*), MONTEVIDEO, URUGUAY. Remember, after World War II Uruguay was considered a safe haven for escaping Nazi's. The Bush family, known for their Nazi's ties, have purchased large ranches in both Uruguay and Paraguay. They may think they can get away with crashing the world economy and hiding out with their stolen loot, but this will never happen, the world must hold these people accountable for their crimes.

This stolen money is now being used for every New World Order pet project imaginable, ranging from NASA, militarized space weapons, electronic mind control, and financial warfare. If you ever wondered where they got the money to build those black project, antigravity vehicles, look no further, as all treaties are classified, "Top Secret".

In 1963, President Kennedy tried to stop this illegal activity and bring this wealth to the people of the world, through the Green Hilton Agreement. This would allow the United States as holders of the International Reserve Currency to print a new gold backed currency using assets from the collateral accounts to boost economic development throughout the world.

On June 4, 1963, President Kennedy signed executive order 11110 which would strip the Federal Reserve Bank of its ability to loan money to the United States with interest, and it required a bullion backed currency issued by the US treasury instead of the Federal Reserve Bank. Soon after, $2 dollar and $5 dollar notes backed by silver were issued that read "United States Note" instead of "Federal Reserve Note".

Certain elements within the world's elite could not let this happen and thus Kennedy had to go. The Green Hilton Agreement and Executive Order 11110 were both signed into law, but shortly after Kennedy's death, was unrecognized by the United States and later other nations of the world.

To curtail these illegal activities, in 1995 the **Trillenium Trilateral** (*Try-part-tite*) **Commission** was stripped of its power and placed under the control of the United Nations. The collateral accounts now remain under the supervision of Saint Germian and Dr. Tsai Cheng Lee of Nationalist China under the **Office of International Treasury Control** at the UN*. Despite these actions, the U.S. corporate government, the World Bank, the Bank of International Settlements, and the IMF continue their illegal activities without giving a care for the needs of the people of the world.

*UN Charter Control No: 10-60847

In international finance there is a term known as Arbitrage, which allows one to profit in a short period of time from rolling money over and over again. This has allowed the robber barons and illuminati elitists to generate enormous amounts of wealth, by raping the world of its assets through either insider trading or by manufacturing money using fractional reserve banking.

When a banker is licensed to create money through fractional reserve banking they have been given the right to create money out of thin air. This occurs when a bank loans out a proportion of their assets at a rate of say, 1 to 10. In other words, a bank must have one dollar of deposits on their balance sheet for every nine dollars of loans. The other 9/10ths is simply manufactured out of thin air. After the debt is paid in full, the banks simply delete this money from their ledgers causing it to vanish from thin air.

But because the interest portion of this debt is not issued into the money supply, there isn't enough money available to repay all the debts, which will exponentially grow into a larger and larger debt bubble. And during this time, the bankers will exchange their worthless fiat money with no intrinsic value for all physical assets until the day the debt bubble bursts allowing them to foreclose on the entire world.

While the masses were enslaved under fractional reserve banking, the elites were profiting handsomely. By using the power of leverage a bank can bring in a 63% annual profit margin assuming a conservative lending ratio of 1 to 10 and an interest rate of 7%. In this example, a bank has $10 million dollars of deposits and $90 million dollars of loans. At an interest rate of 7% this $90 million loan portfolio can bring in $6.3 million dollars annually. However, this example does not account for the carry trade or fancy derivatives which could further enhance earnings in excess of 300% annually.

Wealthy investors are able to tap into these profits by investing in bank trades which are conducted on a monthly basis. At the end of each month, money is then rolled again thus giving it the name of the **"Bank Roll" programs**. The prosperity funds which originated from confiscated accounts taken from the Federal Reserve were also placed into these bankroll programs, but more about this later.

Today there are at least 72 bank roll programs, including (*Bur-ja-vene*) Bergavine, Savage, SBC Chorcoe, ITI, Morgan, Hong Kong, Omega, and Freedom. They are maintained and audited by Price-Waterhouse, the IMF, and the **Treasury of the Republic of the United States** and are deposited in IMF controlled offshore banks. The reason you may have never heard of these secretive trading programs is because investors are required to have a minimum of a $100 million dollars or more just to make a trade.

Any enquiries about these programs are deflected, and attention is instead focused on the warnings issued by government agencies about fake programs. When combined with numerous prosecutions of fraudulent High Yield Investment transactions that occur each year, the public is led to believe that these programs do not exist.

Around the turn of the century some of the wealthy robber baron children placed aside a small amount of their families' money within these programs to be used for the benefit of all people in the world. These wealthy investors are known as wealthy visionaries or **white knights**.

In the early 1990's they invited a few wealthy multiple level marketers to open up an "accumulator account" at the IMF, allowing them to make a bank trade within the bank roll programs with less money. But this was a big mistake and soon word of these programs began to spread, allowing any investor to invest in these bank roll programs with as little as $100. These small amounts were handled by trustees, who collected the money and kept records, and combined the small investments into a larger amount such as one million dollars that was required to enter a "roll".

These "accumulator accounts" were eventually closed to new investors in the late 1990's. However, the original investors are still waiting to be paid because payment can only be made with a gold backed currency, otherwise the Federal Reserve bankers would just steal the money under the current fiat credit system.

The bankers, angry that the bank rolls programs were found out by the people, fought long and hard to stop the programs from funding. Even though thousands of people had invested money and a great deal of wealth was generated, little, if anything was ever paid back to the investors. Corruption, greed, and murder became wide spread among the bankers, government, and even some trustees; who stole the money for themselves. Program managers were lied to, bribed, and many were hauled into court under false pretenses; such as trustees Clyde Hood and Mike Kadoski. Some investors were offered their money back, but most refused to accept payment because they did not trust the government.

TO BE CONTINUED IN PART II…(Credit Roll)

Change Is On The Horizon

PART II
The American Federal Empire

Since the fall of Atlantis, Satan and his minions have been working tirelessly to end all goodness on this planet. But God and the brotherhood of light had put together their own plan to defeat the dark side. Throughout history many prophets come forth to speak of the coming of a golden age of humanity. This truth was made known, only to fall silent on the deaf ears of the ignorant masses. But **change is on the horizon**, a dark day is about to unfold.

To understand how the world got into this mess, we must now travel back in time to the very founding of the American republic. Prior the Revolutionary War the American colonies had grown quite prosperous with full employment in a very short period of time. When King George the third asked Benjamin Franklin the secret of this success, Franklin responded.

"It is because, in the Colonies, we issue our own paper money. We call it Colonial Script, and we issue only enough to move all goods freely from the producers to the Consumers; and as we create our money, we control the purchasing power of money, and have no interest to pay." But the King was jealous of the success of the colonies and their paper based fiat money system which was not backed by precious metals.

Life in Georgian England was an entirely different story; high taxation meant the prisons were filled with debtors and the streets were filled with unemployed beggars with little hope of escape. The taxes paid to the king barely covered the interest payment on the debts he owed to Mayer Amschel Rothschild.

With the wealthy in England overtaxed, King George turned to the colonists by requiring all taxes to be paid in gold coins rather than colonial script. Since the colonists had very little gold; unemployment and cries for war soon surfaced. Benjamin Franklin later said this was the true cause of war not the tax on tea or the stamp act as taught in the history books, over and over again.

Violent opposition soon broke out forcing King George to send English soldiers to enforce the new taxes. When these troops refused to fire on British citizens, the king agreed to let Mayer Rothschild purchase German Hessian troops as mercenary fighters dressed in British uniforms to collect his debt for him. When it became clear these Hessian troops could not successfully defeat the continental army, King George finally relinquished and said, "We may have lost the colony, but we will get her back."

To bring the colonists to their knees, Mayer Rothschild proposed a novel idea; he would loan money to the continental army, through British Rothschild agents in France, in order to control them. From that point on, England stopped trying to "divide and **conquer**" America through force; but instead chose to **retake** her colonies through the stealth of "divide and **control**". To implement this new policy he recruited a network of British spies still loyal to the crown to infiltrate and guide the new republic's government into the hands of British bankers.

In 1788, before the United States even existed, British war loans were now coming due. Because the federal government had no significant financial resources to pay these loans they declared bankruptcy and placed the debt on the states instead of the people.

To make the war debt pending against the people, in 1790 congress passed "An Act making provision for the payment of the Debt of the United States." This Act abolished **states of the republic** and created **federal districts** in their place. A portion of the war debt was then placed on each one of these **districts**, soon after all the states and citizens were reorganized as **corporations** and as a corporation you are not subject to the bill rights. This may explain why you feel like you have no rights under the Constitution it's because you don't, you are not subject to it.

Even though the colonists had removed British troops from their land, they were now at the mercy of British bankers. After defaulting on their war debts, one of President Washington first acts in power was to declare a **financial emergency**. Desperate for funds, the United States allowed the creation of a **private central bank** controlled by the Bank of England and the Rothschild family, by pledging the assets and securities of the United States as collateral.

Despite the protests of the Democrats and Republicans lead by Thomas Jefferson, Washington recruited the aid of Alexander Hamilton who was Secretary of Treasury and a Rothschild agent, to draft a proposal which in 1791 became the **Bank of the United States**. And just like the Bank of

England, which was also privately owned, the Bank of the United States was named in such a way as to conceal its true ownership.

This bank was given a 20 year charter and capitalized with $10,000,000 dollars, 80% of which was owned by foreign bankers. Using fractional reserve banking the bank was authorized to loan out twice as much money as it had in reserves, or $20,000,000. This made a profitable enterprise for the bankers, as they could collect interest on an extra $10,000,000 dollars that was simply manufactured out of thin air.

By 1796, the national debt of the United States government had grown to $6.2 million dollars, forcing the government to sell most of *its own* shares in the Bank of the United States. By 1802, the government owned *no stock* in its own Bank.

With the outbreak of the Napoleonic Wars in Europe, in 1803, the relationship between the United States and Great Britain had begun to deteriorate. Britain had imposed a blockade on all neutral countries, including the United States. During this time Britain was *taking* American sailors as hostages from their ships to serve in the British Navy.

In response to this increasing infiltration of troublemakers, and a host of British spies within the United States, Congress passed an amendment which prevented anyone who held titles of nobility or connections to the Crown of England from holding public office, such as Esquire-Attorney, Doctor, and Clergyman. These titles were authorized under the Crown of England for English Citizens and thus these holders are foreign agents of the Crown.

The Titles of Nobility Amendment, also known as the 13th Amendment, was approved by Congress and the House of Representatives, in 1810. It was ratified by all the necessary states into law, on March 12, 1819. It reads as follows . . .

"If any citizen of the United States shall accept, claim, receive or retain, any title of nobility or honour, or shall, without the consent of Congress, accept and retain any present, pension, office or emolument of any kind whatever, from any emperor, king, prince or foreign power, such person shall cease to be a citizen of the United States, and shall be incapable of holding any office of trust or profit under them, or either of them." — Titles of Nobility Amendment 1810.

After the passage of the Titles of Nobility Amendment Congress went one step further by severing British control over the financial system, when they refused to renew the First United States Bank Charter which expired on February 20, 1811. Nathan Mayer Rothschild was quoted as saying "Either the application for renewal of the Charter is granted, or the United States will find itself involved in a most disastrous war."

When it became apparent that the United States would not go along with the bankers schemes; Rothschild responded "Teach those impudent Americans a lesson; bring them back to colonial status."

In retaliation for refusing to do business on their terms, **European investors** withdrew $7,000,000 in specie or coin money from the U.S. economy; resulting in an economic recession and the eventual outbreak of the War of 1812.

The causes of the War of 1812 were triggered by England's loss of control over the United States monetary system, and even more worrisome, the Titles of Nobility Amendment prevented British agents from meddling in the affairs of the new republic's government. So England ordered their soldiers to burn down Washington D.C.

With the White House and the Library of Congress now in flames, evidence of the original Titles of Nobility Amendment was destroyed. The British Crown knew the American people would no longer tolerate British rule again, so they returned the republic back to the people **with one exception,** the 13th amendment was to be removed from the Constitution. This amendment began disappearing from texts in 1832, and by 1876 was removed from all official state publications thanks to extreme bribery from the Rothschild banking syndicate. Proof that the 13th amendment was ratified was found in 1983 by archive researcher David Dodge and Tom Dunn, in a rural Maine library.

After the War of 1812, English bankers, such as the Rothschild's, sought to recapture the American economy. They knew that if they could control the money supply they would not care who created the laws. Thanks to all the new war debt which needed financing, they got their wish when President James Madison granted a charter to the **Second National Bank**, in 1816.

But this bank was laced with political corruption, as they would often purchase politicians by funding their election campaigns. The newly elected President, Andrew Jackson, responded to their mischief with these famous words . . .

"You are a den of vipers and thieves. I intend to rout you out, and by the eternal God I will rout you out."

After a failed assassination attempt, he told his close friend and the future President, Martin Van Buren, "The bank, is trying to kill me, but I will kill it!"

In 1832, Andrew Jackson vetoed a renewal of the banks charter on the grounds that the bank was unconstitutional. He successfully paid off the National Debt, for the first time in the nation's history, with a surplus of $5,000 dollars. After the bank charter had expired the books were opened up, and Congress was shocked to learn that every single stock holder was a British citizen!

On January 30, 1835, President Andrew Jackson attended a congressional funeral in the capitol building, as he exited, Richard Lawrence fired a pistol at Jackson, but the percussion cap exploded and the bullet would not discharge. So an enraged Jackson strikes his cane against the attacker, who then fires another bullet, which also failed to discharge.

Jackson later claims the Rothschild's were responsible for this incident.

In 1857, the Illuminati met in London to decide America's fate. They knew that if they could incite an expensive and costly war, then the United States would be forced to charter a central bank. But because Canada and Mexico were too weak to fight a war; and England, France, and Russia were too far away, they decided to foment a civil war between the North and South. The North was to become a British colony, annexed to Canada under the control of **Lionel Rothschild**, and the South with its valuable cotton industry was to be given to Napoleon III of France, to be controlled by **James Rothschild**.

By the 1860's, slavery was gradually becoming obsolete thanks to increased education and changing of attitudes. But the Illuminati capitalized on the racial tensions in order to **"Divide and Control" America** through civil war. Albert Pike, the head of both the Masonic and illuminati Orders, recruited the help of the Knights of the Golden Circle, which was formed in 1854, by George Bickley. Their members included a 'who's who' of notable people, including the President of the Confederate States, Jefferson Davis, John Wilkes Booth, and the infamous bank robber, Jesse James, whose operations helped fund the Civil War. Later in 1867, the Knights of the Golden Circle spun-off the Ku Klux Klan.

In 1861, Lincoln approached the Rothschild controlled banks in New York to raise money for the Civil War. After they quoted him an insane usurious interest rate of 24% to 36%, Lincoln ordered the US treasury to print the money, debt free. In 1972, the US Treasury Department computed that this move saved the government nearly $4 billion dollars of interest.

These debt free notes, backed by precious metals, were known as "Greenbacks," due to the green colored ink printed on the back. During the course of the war, and later during the reconstruction era that soon followed, over $449 million ($449,338,902) dollars were issued, bringing both value and stability to the war torn republic, and to help restore constitutional control over the money supply.

In response to the greenbacks, Lincoln once said, "We gave the people of this Republic the greatest blessing they have ever had; their own paper money to pay their own debts."

The Civil War created many challenges for Lincoln, but some of his mistakes are still haunting us, to this day, in particular the early foundation of a **shadow government**, and the **true meaning** of a 14th amendment citizen.

The concept of a shadow government within the United States first began on March 27, 1861, when the southern states walked out of Congress. Because there were not enough members present in Congress to conduct a legislative session, under the rules of parliamentary law, the only lawful authority they had to vote on a time to reconvene for a new session. But instead of agreeing on a new time to reassemble, they choose to abandoned Congress altogether.

This created a constitutional crisis which placed Congress in (sign-na die-eh) sine die, which literally means "without day". In (*Sign-na die-eh*) sine die, congress was no longer a lawful body; and therefore they could no longer declare war under a constitutional authority. In addition, the Constitution for the United States had ceased to exist when parties from the southern states had ceded from the union and because the northern states had declared their own state legislatures, in (*Sign-na die-eh*) sine die.

In response to the constitutional crisis, on April 15, 1861, Lincoln signed an executive order, known as **Executive**

Proclamation 1, which declared a **"National Emergency"** and placed the federal territories under martial law, to be ruled by executive powers. Because the federal government within the district of Columbia did not have any jurisdiction in the state territories, on April 24, 1863, he commissioned **General Orders No. 100**, also known as **The Lieber Code**, to extend the laws of the District of Columbia beyond the boundaries of Washington D.C., into the several states, placing all Americans under the **military occupation** of the United States government.

After the conclusion of the Civil War, Lincoln intended to end the Lieber Code, and return to constitutional law, but his plans were cut short when he was assassinated. As a result **martial law** under a shadow government, continues to this day.

Not only did the Lieber Code enable Lincoln to sidestep the constitutional crisis, but it also allowed him to navigate around Rothschild controlled interests. In 1865, the war was now going badly for Lincoln, when he delivered a message to Congress saying, *"I have two great enemies, the southern army in front of me, and the financial institutions in the rear. Of the two, the one in my rear is my greatest foe."*

In 1862, the Rothschild plans for invasion of the United States was on schedule, when England had stationed 8,000 troops in Canada, and France had stationed 30,000 troops in Mexico. To deal with the Rothschild problem, Lincoln had contacted his friend, Tsar Alexander II of Russia, for military assistance because he too was opposed to a Rothschild controlled central bank in his country, and because Lincoln showed goodwill by emancipating the slaves.

To ensure military victory for the union forces, Tsar Alexander parked his naval fleet in the New York and San Francisco harbor to block any invasion attempts by the English or French. Because of their help, and because the Tsars blocked the creation of a Zionist one world government at the Congress of Vienna in 1815, the Rothschild's had sealed their fate. When sixty years later, the Tsar Dynasty met their own downfall at the hands of Rothschild agents during the Bolshevik Revolution.

By opposing the Rothschild's and by printing the greenbacks, English Bankers signed President Lincoln's death warrant, so they hired John Wilkes Booth to assassinate Lincoln. Sadly, a local vagrant was found nearby, in a hay barn, and was innocently charged and sentenced for the crime. After escaping from his captors, John Wilkes Booth lived out the remainder of his life in comfortable surroundings, in England.

In 1868, the 14th amendment was ratified ending slavery by giving all American's citizenship.

> "All persons born or naturalized in the United States, and subject to the jurisdiction thereof, are citizens of the United States and of the State wherein they reside." — United States Code Annotated Amendment 14.

However, what the public was not told, while under the Lieber Code, a 14th amendment citizen can only be found within the jurisdiction of the United States; that is, all government employees, all those who live in territories occupied by the federal government, such as Washington D.C., and the former slaves. The rest of the population was not subject to the 14ᵗʰ amendment, and thus could still claim jurisdiction under the original Constitution.

In addition to that, after the conclusion to the Civil War the federal government was now occupying the southern states placing these **"captured" citizens** under the jurisdiction of the Lieber code. The southern states had to agree to ratify this amendment in order for them to be granted their freedom from federal rule. Thus, instead of ending slavery, the 14ᵗʰ amendment held all southerners captive as slaves in the plantation known as the "United States of America."

Just like how all citizens were turned into corporations in 1790, to subject them to the Revolutionary War debts; 14th amendment citizens were created to be franchisees subject to the corporation known as the "United States, Inc." And like all corporate brands, you do not have any constitutional Bill of Rights protections. Proof of such can be found in the all-caps version of your name, which signifies a corporate entity.

After the Civil War, the United States defaulted on its war debt. During the bankruptcy proceedings, cunning lawyers in league with international bankers found a loophole within Article I, Section 8, Clause 17, of the United States Constitution which allowed the creation of a duplicate entity, known as the corporation of the UNITED STATES OF AMERICA, to replace the now bankrupt and defunct Republic for the United States of America.

"To exercise exclusive legislation in all cases whatsoever, over such District (not exceeding ten miles square) as may, by cession of particular

states, and the acceptance of Congress, become the seat of the government of the United States, and to exercise like authority over all places purchased by the consent of the legislature of the state in which the same shall be, for the erection of forts, magazines, arsenals, dockyards, and other needful buildings . . ." — *Article I, Section 8, Clause 17.*

This occurred with the passage of **"The District of Columbia Organic Act of 1871"** which incorporated the area of the District of Columbia into a **private foreign corporation**, charted in the city of London, known as **UNITED STATES, INC**. This corporation designated Congress as the **board of directors** to continue the business needs of the government, under martial law. Thanks to the Lieber code, federal jurisdiction under the Organic Act was expanded to include not only all captured citizens in the southern states but all Americans in all states. Thus, America had lost her sovereignty under the yoke of the Crown of England and the International Bankers.

During this same time, the corporation of the United States adopted its *own* constitution which was identical to the original national constitution. To fool the people, one word was changed from its original form:

The Constitution **for** the **u**nited states of America.

To its present day **all capitalized form** which signifies a corporate entity:

THE CONSTITUTION **OF** THE **U**NITED STATES OF AMERICA.

Incidentally, the Titles of Nobility Amendment was removed from this new constitution.

With illuminati in full control over the United States they now sought to rule the world. After the death of Adam (wise-hoff) Weishaupt in 1830, (*Jew-zehp-peh*) Giuseppe Mazzini was selected to head the illuminati. In 1871, the mantle of power was passed on again to the American, general Albert Pike as its new director. Pike became fascinated with the idea of a one world government and eventually constructed the Illuminati's blueprint of world domination.

His plans called for the financing of **three world wars** in 20th century. The first war would bring about an **atheist communist state** from the ashes of Tsarist Russia. The second war would bring about a **Jewish holocaust under a fascist government** to foment support of a Zionist state of Israel. The third war would manipulate the **differences of Christians and Muslims** for their own annihilation. Then finally, **political Zionism** would come out as victors of all.

These three world wars would require enormous funding. Since most of the royalty in Europe was already deeply in debt, thanks to the numerous wars and conflicts created by the Rothschild banking dynasty, the only place left that could possibly pay for such ambitious plans was the now prosperous **American Republic**.

After the civil war, the United States went through a great industrial expansion. The new industries of oil, steel, textile, and railroad all needed generous financing which the Rothschild family was more than eager to provide. To access these markets, the Rothschild's sent their agent

Jacob Schiff to infiltrate the New York banking scene; which was controlled by J.P. Morgan.

By the turn of the century, the Rothschild's had fully entrenched themselves into the **tight fraternity** of Wall Street banks such as Goldman-Sachs and Lehman Brothers. They now sought their most prized possession, full control over the American monetary system. With help from Jacob Schiff and J.P. Morgan, the Rothschild's formed a scheme which would seduce Congress into relinquishing control over the money supply.

This occurred with the **Panic of 1907** when a liquidity crisis caused many banks and business to fail all across the United States. The meltdown began when J.P. Morgan published rumors that the Knickerbocker Trust Company of New York was insolvent. With a bank run on hand, they were forced to call in their loans creating a chain reaction which would threaten to implode the entire banking system. The failures continued until J.P. Morgan and Company provided a generous loan to the insolvent banks. But J.P. Morgan was not trying to **save** the American banking system, but rather, he used the crisis to **destroy** his competition by choosing which banks he would bailout.

But the biggest causality of the economic fallout was the **looming bankruptcy** of the Corporation of the United Sates which had no means to pay back their loans which were due in 1912. In anticipation of this bankruptcy, representatives from the world's most powerful families met in November 1910, at a secret meeting at the Jekyll Island Club Resort in Georgia to discuss the foreclosure of the **corporation of the United States** and to brainstorm solutions which would prevent future liquidity crises such as occurred during the Panic of 1907.

Those in attendance included Senator Nelson Aldrich, Paul Warburg, representatives from J.P. Morgan and Company, and Jacob Schiff representing the Rothschild family. They proposed a **20 year extension** on the national debt, if the United States would agree to charter a **privately owned central bank**, which would serve as a bank of last resort by lending money to other insolvent banks in order to prevent future bank runs.

A week later they emerged with their plans to create what is now known as the **Federal Reserve System**. Because the current President Taft would never agree to sign away the American monetary system to a cabal of international bankers, they waited until they got their man, the progressive Woodrow Wilson into power. In return for the banker's generous campaign contributions, Woodrow Wilson reluctantly promised the bankers he would sign the **Federal Reserve Act** if he was elected into office.

Many powerful forces were opposed to the creation of a privately controlled central bank. To neutralize this threat, J.P. Morgan invited the major opponents of the Federal Reserve Act onboard the maiden voyage of the newly built **Titanic luxury streamliner** built by the White Star Line, owned by J.P. Morgan. J.P. Morgan ordered the captain to steer his ship into an iceberg, and under gunpoint prevented the men from escaping onto the lifeboats, killing many his enemies in one large swoop. When word of this got back to Woodrow Wilson, he commented, "There exists this power in the world so subtle, so organized, so watchful, that we dare not speak above a whisper when we speak in condemnation of it."

At the beginning of 1913, the United States had defaulted on its debt. After being denied a new line of credit, the now President, Woodrow Wilson, faced a constitutional crisis. With no other sources of funding he went along with the bankers schemes engineered at the Jekyll Island Resort.

To avoid any opposition, Senator Nelson Aldrich quickly pushed the Federal Reserve Act through both houses of Congress. On December 23, 1913, while most of Congress was away on Christmas vacation, a quorum call was issued. A few selected congressional traitors voted by voice to avoid public record and passed the Federal Reserve Act, which President Wilson signed into law. Wilson later admitted with remorse, when referring to the Fed, "I have unwittingly ruined my country".

This act gave away the keys of the printing presses at the U.S. treasury **to a foreign corporation**, chartered under the Crown of England known as the **Federal Reserve Bank**. The Federal Reserve Bank advertises itself as a non-profit corporation that operates as if it's another branch of the government. However, its board members are unelected and their meetings are conducted behind closed doors away from public scrutiny. All this secrecy becomes very suspicious considering how the Federal Reserve monitors and controls trillions of dollars within the world's banking system.

After the federal government lost its ability to issue its own money, the national debt soon soared to astronomical heights. Because, now the government had to pay the

Federal Reserve **interest** on all its currency printed into circulation. But this interest on the National Debt could never be repaid as the Federal Reserve required **all debts to be repaid with gold**, which the government did not have. And even worse, the **interest portion** of the national debt was not issued into the money supply. In other words more and more debt will have to be issued to continue servicing the growing interest payments on all loans.

In order to cover this interest payment, Congress was forced to pass the income tax legislation, which became law in 1913, with the ratification of 16th amendment; also known as the **income tax amendment**. Initially they levied a 1% *voluntary tax* on all incomes over $3,000, and a *progressive surtax* on incomes over $20,000, but this would soon increase with the outbreak of World War I and World War II.

Income tax allowed the Federal Reserve System to confiscate the earnings of the common man. But the industrialists and financers were exempted from paying any income tax because they could afford to hide their assets in **tax free foundations** which they claimed were devoted to philanthropy. Examples of such include the Rockefeller Foundation, the Mellon Foundation, and the Carnegie Endowment.

Technically, the 16th amendment was not ratified by the necessary states as it violates the constitutional clause of **no direct taxes**. Despite this; Congress went ahead and taxed the people anyway. The government was able to do this because under their corporate charter, Congress was operating as the **board of directors** and therefore they had the authority to enter this amendment **as ratified**. But remember, this amendment has nothing to do with the original United States Constitution, which was replaced back in 1871 with the corporate constitution.

"No capitation, or other direct tax, shall be laid, unless in proportion to the census or enumeration herein before directed to be taken." — Article I, Section 9, Clause 4.

In 1933, the United States once again declared bankruptcy. To make all citizens subject to the repayment on the National Debt, the bankers chartered a **Delaware corporation** known as the **Bureau of Internal Revenue**. But this corporation was illegally masquerading as part of the government, placing them under a constant threat of lawsuit. To escape this ligation, they moved their jurisdiction **outside** of the United States, to Puerto Rico. This occurred in 1953* when they changed their name to the **"Internal Revenue Service"** or **"IRS"** incorporated as a **Puerto Rican Trust** within the division of the **Department of the Treasury of the Commonwealth of Puerto Rico**. Further proof can be found within the United States Code which lists the IRS as **Trust fund #62**, the Puerto Rico special fund (**Internal Revenue**). This was done to divert all income tax payments to the **International Monetary Fund** owned by the various central banks of Europe and North America, which in turn are owned by the Crown of England.

Revenue Agent:
Any duly authorized Commonwealth Internal Revenue Agent of the Department of the Treasury of Puerto Rico.
27 CFR 26.11
Puerto Rico special fund (Internal Revenue).
Section 31 U.S.C. 1321(a)(62)

*See **Reorganization Plan 26 of 1950 and Reorganization Plan 1 of 1952**, both mandated by Harry Truman.*

The evidence proving income tax is paid to the United Kingdom is found deep within the IRS Individual Master File, which contains every transaction and financial record gathered by IRS officials throughout your lifetime. One of these codes (**300-399 blocking series**) determines what kind of tax you are paying. After looking this code up within the **IRS 6209 Manual**, you find that they have incorrectly classified all Americans as **domiciled corporations** in either Guam, the Virgin Islands, or Puerto Rico (**IRS 6209 Manual "TC 150"**). Furthermore, all taxpayers who filled out a 1040 form (**IMF 300-309, Barred Assessment, CP 55 generated valid for MFT-30**) are subject to a tax for doing commerce with the United Kingdom under a treaty with the United States (**Business Master File BMF 390-399 reads U.S.-U.K. Tax Treaty Claims**). As you follow the money trail you find that the taxes collected on the **1040 Form** is then sent to the Crown of England as a tribute payment.

The Crown of England is a **sovereign corporation** located within the 677 acres of **"The City"** found within the heart of greater London. This tiny strip of land contains the world's most power banking houses such as the **Bank of England** and **Lloyd's of London** owned by the House of Rothschild. It is these bankers and their counterpart, the temple bar attorneys, that constitute the **powerbase** known simply as the **"Crown"**.

Even though the queen of England is a member of this club, she is not its corporate head, that job was given to the

Pontiff of Rome. The Pope was given control over the Monarchy with the signing of the Treaty of 1213 between King John and Pope Innocent III, which forever pledged England as a vassal state of the Holy Roman Empire. In 1297, that treaty was used as a precedent to incorporate **"The City"** as an **independent city state** controlled by the Vatican; which would **govern England** without directly relying on the Monarchy.

Just like how the corporation of the United States was subject to the Crown of England, so too were the subjects of the British Empire **enslaved with debt** by the financial division of the Vatican headquartered within the City of London. Today this **small clique of bankers** have full authority over the affairs of Parliament, and this has been the case since 1694, when Pope Innocent XI hired William of Orange to dispose the Stuart Kings and charter the Bank of England.

Located within the Crown of England is the original **Federal Reserve charter** which, according to farmer claims legal team, allocates that 67% of the income tax collected by the IRS was to be divided to the Crown of England, another 23% was to be paid as a **dividend** to the 300 shareholders of the Federal Reserve Bank, and the last 10% was paid to the **employees of the IRS** to keep them quiet about this sweet deal.

Since 1913 none of the income tax collected by the IRS has gone to the federal government. The federal government is funded totally **through black budget sources** such as drug trafficking and off-budget accounting on the **Comprehensive Annual Financial Reports**.

The Comprehensive Annual Financial Report, also known as the CAFR (pronounced 'Calf' –er), was based on techniques first used by the mafia to hide their assets. In 1946, the government adopted the same methods when a private organization known as the **Government Finance Officers Association** (GFOA) created a policy which changed the government from a **"Pay-As-You-Go"** structure into a **"For-Profit"** structure used by corporate America. Soon after, governments began using a **financial statement** which allowed them to create multiple **profit centers** and **investment accounts** and to do it in such a way that the public would never figure out. Over time, the government began to make so much money that they overtook the mafia as the **biggest game in town**.

In 1977, the GFOA spun-off *another* private organization known as the **Government Accounting Standards Board** which promoted the lucrative benefits of a **standardized financial statement**. Soon all local, county, and state governments jumped on board and began producing their own version of either a **Comprehensive Annual Financial Report** (CAFR), an **Annual Financial Report** (AFR), or on the federal level, a **Consolidated Financial Statement** (CFS).

As of 2005 there are over 148,000 individual **government financial statements** in the United States, with a combined local, state and, federal level investment of at least $110 trillion dollars. With so much money, one must ask why the government has any debt at all. To answer this is complex, because the government's debts are **financed indirectly** through their own investment funds. This was done to subject the people to the repayment of the debt while at the same time the government could steal all the wealth of the people.

The CAFR allows the government to **hide their assets** through the use of **two sets** of accounting books. One is the **"Budget Report"** which is presented to the public as the actual budget. The only income that must be reported in government budget reports are taxes, fines, and fees. But this is only a **small image** within the entire financial picture. The other set of accounting books are known as the **FINANCIAL STATEMENTS** of the CAFR, the AFR; and on the federal level, the CFS. These show a more complete financial condition of the government, which includes all the income generated from government Liquid Investment Funds, Bond Financing Accounts, and Corporate Stock Portfolios. Some examples of these investment centers include self insurance, enterprise operations, self debt funding accounts; hundreds if not thousands of specialty funding accounts, creatively enacted advance forward liability accounts, federally Funded program accounts, pensions, real estate venture projects, and property seized by the state.

When you look into these funds, you find governments have actually been stashing away large surpluses of money from the general public. These funds have been kept away from the taxpayer, while taxes are raised, and citizens told to expect fewer services. None of these **revenue centers** report their income in the general budget, allowing the government to hide how much money they are truly making, within each accounting cycle, and it serves to create a **void of comprehension** keeping the public in the dark of what is truly going on. If a private sector business was to adopt these same accounting practices they would qualify as a **criminal enterprise**, under the **RICO statutes for extortion**. But the government wiggled around this by passing laws designed to **elude all consequences** of their theft.

RICO

*The **Racketeer Influenced and Corrupt Organizations Act** was designed to fight organized crime and investigate and prosecute individuals conspiring to participate in racketeering.*

Which is another part of the problem. Today over 70% to 80% of all elected officials are associated with the **massive attorney network complex** which has since taken over the three branches of the government. These attorneys make laws which give them the power to sue anyone who dares attempt to access these funds. As long as people continue voting these attorneys into office they will continue **stealing these massive profits** for themselves.

When analyzing the total income generated on a composite level of local, state, and federal government financial statements, the non-disclosed revenues now account for 66% of all the government's income, while the other 33% is still derived from tax revenues. If the government's administrative duties were modified slightly, through the creation of **Tax Retirement Funds**, then the profits generated could easily run all governments without any further need of taxation, and still have enough money left over to pay a **<u>dividend check</u>** to every American.

TRF funds would be set up like a pension fund but with the goal of retiring all forms of taxation. The majority of its investments would be made to local businesses, stimulating their own local economy, instead of Wall Street and offshore banks. After auditing and applying surpluses found within the CAFR; most governments have half the funds needed to create a **Tax Retirement Fund**, the other half could be raised over a five year period using income generated in various CAFR **revenue centers**. Eventually the funds will grow large enough to phase out all taxation, creating thriving local economies, and even greater sums of money for all people.

According to the research uncovered by concerned activist, Walter Burien the editor of the **cafr1.com** website, in 1998, the federal government collected $1.8 trillion dollars in taxes and all local and state governments collected $1.6 trillion, with total tax revenues of $3.5 trillion. The revenue centers found within the CAFR brought in another $5.1 trillion, with a grand total of $8.5 trillion dollars of gross income for the government. And according to the World Bank, the United States economy generated only $8.7 trillion dollars for that same year. But this statistic is misleading because the income generated by the government is **excluded from the GDP** to hide the fact that the government makes more revenue than general population. If this data was revised to show all private and public sector income, then the total GDP in 1998 would have been $17.2 trillion dollars; with the government accounting for 49% of all economic activity within the United States. By the year 2009, this number has since grown to nearly 70% of all economic activity; leaving little doubt the United States is now a **command economy**.

But even more alarming, these non-disclosed government **investment funds** have become so massive they now control 60% to 70% of all American corporations. Whenever you hear about these so-called **"institutional investors"** mentioned in the news media, they are actually referring to a composite of governmental **pension funds** and domestic and international **specialty funds**, which in the year of 2000, accounted for an 82% stock ownership of Microsoft, 61% of Disney, 58% of AOL-Time Warner, and 72% of EXXON. But of course the **government owned news media** would never dare report these numbers to the American people.

With such a large sum of money at their disposal the stock and bond markets are regularly manipulated making or breaking any corporation which does not follow the New World Order agenda. No wonder we feel like the stock market is rigged, because it is. This also explains why the **"government-owned" news media** will not report any thing critical of the government, and also why the government has no intentions of reforming the profitable **government owned** health care industry.

But even *more frightening,* by using the power of **proxy vote,** the government can force corporate America to do its own bidding. This explains why we have so much off-shoring. Back in the 1960's, most of the businesses owned within the CAFR were primarily restricted to American owned corporations. But in 1978, the government side-stepped this rule by creating **international investment pools** which began taking over companies overseas, in order to make huge profits from cheaper labor, and in turn putting Americans out of work. Sadly corporate leaders are powerless to do anything about this lest their companies would be destroyed, or even worse, things could happen to them, such as the government firing the **entire board of directors** and replacing them with their own cronies.

Off-shoring has also allowed these same companies to hide their income from the IRS by setting up **domicile corporations** throughout the world like in the Cayman Islands. Today, the largest American corporations such as found within the Fortune 500 pay a paltry sum of .02% to 1.5% income tax after deductions, yet the average American is forced to shell out to their slave masters an average of 27% of their personal income tax returns.

In addition to off-shoring American jobs, the federal and local government has been implicated in using its derivatives to **manipulate financial markets** throughout the world. According to a March 2008, US Treasury audit of its bank derivative holdings, the government currently holds over $180 trillion dollars of **derivatives** most of which are held within the five largest American banks. These **credit swaps derivatives** are used to manipulate all commodity prices including the short and long term bond yields, the prices of crude oil, precious metals, and stock certificates. Creating easy money for the government but consequently leading to a speculative **global bubble market** and its eventual demise. Which seems to be what they want, **to drain all the people's assets** in a covert and hidden way; while inevitably enhancing the profits of their own investments funds. To correct this problem, a full audit of the government's financial statements must be disclosed to the public, but as long as attorneys continue to monopolize the functions of the government, it's doubtful this will ever happen.

*Derivative: A **financial contract** whose value is derived from the **performance** of underlying market factors.*

While the theft of the people's money continued to impoverish the masses, the lucrative printing presses at the Federal Reserve Bank managed to enslave them; bringing the New World Order one step closer to reality.

Through the magic of fractional reserve banking the Federal Reserve System can create or destroy money. But because the **interest portion** of the banks loaning activity is not issued into the money supply, more and more loans are necessarily to continue financing debt, and to continue injecting money into the economy creating a **debt bubble** that can only grow larger and larger. During this time, physical assets are exchanged as collateral for intangible fiat money until the day the **debt bubble bursts** allowing the bankers to foreclose on the entire world.

The founding fathers were well aware of this danger, which is why they outlawed the use of **privately issued fiat money** as according to Article I, Section 10 of the Constitution which mandates that **debts can only be repaid** with gold and silver.

"No State shall... coin Money; emit Bills of Credit; make any Thing but gold and silver Coin a Tender in Payment of Debt." — Article I, Section 10, Clause 1, the United States constitution.

In 1971, Nixon illegally stripped all Federal Reserve Notes from the gold standard, and ever since, Americans have been using unlawful money. Without the backing of precious metals, these notes would not even be considered money, as money has intrinsic value. Federal Reserve notes are technically **certificates of debt** as they can only be issued into the money supply through the **loaning activity** of fractional reserve banking. When you take a closer look at a dollar bill you see the words.

"This note is legal tender for all debts, public and private." But one needs to ask themselves, *to whom this debt is owed?*

The bankers were able to get around the Constitution's restriction of fiat money by using a clause within section 16 of the Federal Reserve Act which stipulates that **Federal Reserve Notes can only be used by Federal Reserve Banks**. Isn't it amazing that the bankers consider all the people who use their privately issued credit to be **Federal Reserve Banks**?

And with Federal Reserve's **open check book**, stock markets can be manipulated creating even greater sums of money for the bankers. And even worse, they now had the finances to bankroll **World War I** and **World War II**, which helped served as a **diversion** to keep the public unaware of what was really going on.

After the Federal Reserve's takeover of the American monetary system, the bankers could print as much fiat money as they wanted to **buy out anyone** and anything which opposed the New World order agenda. Soon all the major media conglomerates began to fall under their control.

According to a report* given to Congress in 1917, by Congressman Oscar Callaway. In 1915, J.P. Morgan met with 12 high ranking news mangers to determine the most influential newspapers in America and to figure how many of them it would take to generally control the policy of the daily press within the United States. After agreeing it would require the control of 25 of the greatest newspapers, J.P. Morgan, the Rothschild family, and John D. Rockefeller began buying up these papers and replacing them with new editor's who would spread their ideas of a One World Government in a postwar world.

*U.S. Congressional Record February 9, 1917, page 2947.

To help define this new policy the now elderly Jacob Schiff, recruited J.P. Morgan's personal attorney, Elihu Root, and President Wilson's closest advisor, Edward House, to create a **front group** which, in 1921, would become the **Council of Foreign Relations**. Their ranks soon swelled to over 1,000 members representing the heads of virtually every **industrial empire** in America. Soon, other groups similar to the CFR were founded in other nations, such as the **Bilderberg Group** and the **Trilateral Commission**.

Their inner circle of members now conspired to purchase any asset which was not owned by them. And with the Federal Reserve's power of printing, loaning, or withdrawing money, they were able to profit from the **artificially created** boom and bust cycles caused by the feds manipulation of the interest rates which resulted in either inflation or deflation of the money supply. This is why the stock market crashed in 1929.

In the 'roaring twenties' the fed loaned easy money to the public creating a boom period, but in 1929 these loans were **'called in'** artificially reducing the money supply and forcing people into bankruptcy. However, members of the elite were able to get out of the stock market before the crash thanks to an **insider tip** from Paul Warburg who served as both chairman of the CFR and advisor to the Federal Reserve.

By 1930 the fallout of the Great Depression had begun to spread worldwide, resulting in the bankruptcy of numerous countries **including the United States**. In 1933, the **20 year extension** of the national debt, which was extended by Woodrow Wilson in exchange for signing the Federal Reserve act, **was now coming due**. With little hope this debt could ever be repaid the United States now faced *another* looming bankruptcy. Concerned that the dollar would be devalued, Americans began redeeming their Federal Reserve notes for gold and silver.

One of the first things the newly elected President, Franklin D. Roosevelt, did while in office was to stop the **gold redemptions** by declaring the corporation of the United States, bankrupt. This occurred on March 9, 1933, with the passage of the **Emergency Banking Act**, which closed all US banks for four days in order to **reorganize** the insolvent monetary system.

On April 5th, 1933, President Roosevelt signed into law the **Gold Confiscation Act** (Presidential Executive Order 6102).

(Listen to audio clip here.)

The **Gold Confiscation Act** allowed the federal government to confiscate all the people's gold and to remove the gold standard, replacing all currency with **"legal tender" Federal Reserve notes** which could still be redeemed with silver. But in 1968, silver was also removed from circulation and later in 1971, the gold window, set up at the **Bretton Woods agreement,** would also be closed.

1968 $40.06
1969 $41.51
1970 $36.41
1971 $41.25
1972 $58.42

Under the **Bretton Woods agreement** the IMF mandated that the price of gold would be set at a value of $42.22 dollars per ounce of gold. During this time **only foreigners** could redeem the United States dollar for gold. But by August 1971, inflation had sent the market price of gold well above this set level, resulting in massive redemptions of gold by foreign creditors, who exchanged their **devalued dollar** for the more valuable gold stored in the United States **IMF trust fund**.

(Clip of Nixon here)

After President Nixon illegally removed the convertibility of gold and silver from the dollar, Federal Reserve notes have since devalued 81%.

After President Roosevelt confiscated the peoples gold, he changed a provision within the **1917 Trading with the Enemy Act** which redefined all U.S. citizens as **"Enemies of the State"**. Thus the corporate government declared war on its own people. This gave FDR the power to indefinitely maintain a bank holiday preventing any more redemption of Federal Reserve Notes for gold and silver.

Chapter 106, Section 2, subdivision (c), and the Trading with the Enemy Act of 1933, Chapter 106, Section 5, subdivision (b), — Use pictures of US Code at Cornell University's website.

And even worse, every president since the Roosevelt administration has continued to use the **Trading with the Enemies Act** to maintain states of **"national emergency"**. Therefore new conflicts are encouraged to maintain control over the people. This gave President Truman a precedent to sign the **National Security Act of 1947**, which created a **National Security State** with the establishment of the **CIA** and **NSA**.

In 1935, President Roosevelt signed the **Federal Register Act** which gave the president dictatorial powers by allowing him to create any law, without consulting Congress, by simply **publishing them** in the Federal Registry.

By 1938 the *Supreme Court had ratified Roosevelt's emergency banking proclamations which changed the **Constitutional Republic** into a **Legislative Democracy**. "Public **law**" was replaced with "Public **Policy**" and "**Merchant** Law" with "**Admiralty** Law", suspending the Constitution. Legislative language was used which said "Only the President can declare an end to the Emergency". But once in office, and made aware of their dictatorial powers, no President since FDR has been willing to declare an end to the Emergency and return our country to **Constitutional Law**.

*Erie R.R. v Tompkins

The US Constitution allows for three types of laws, **Common** Law such as 'We the People', **Contract** Law governing contracts and agreements, and **Admiralty** Law which governs naval forces on the high seas using military tribunals instead of the constitution and bill of rights. Only in times of war can the President **expand** Admiralty Law within the interior of the United States. This occurred on December 16, 1950, at the beginning of the Korean War when President Truman declared a **National Emergency*** which continues to this day. At that point, gold fringe flags of the Commander-in-Chief began to creep up within the courts, public places, and even churches.

* Proclamation 2914 - December 16, 1950.

Because of the *1933 bankruptcy, the government could no longer receive any more loans from the bankers to continue its operations. So they created an ingenious plan, they would borrow **against the labor** of all 14th amendment citizens. They did this by creating a **Foreign Situs** Trust ** using your **incorporated name** and **birth certificate** as collateral for new loans.

Your Birth Certificate is not owned by you; the **original** is kept by the government which proceeds to issue a **copy of live birth** only. Since the government owns your birth certificate you are considered to be an **employee** of the **corporation** of the United States***. After the state receives your birth certificate it is then **registered** within the **U.S. Department of Transportation** who then has the U.S. Treasury issue a **bond**; using your future labor as **collateral** which guarantees the Federal Reserve System repayment of the **national debt**. It is these bonds that allow the government to continue **borrowing** unlimited money under its full faith and credit scheme.

The government then subjected each person to a **proportion** of the national debt which today runs around $1 million dollars**** per American. This money was then deposited each person's **prepaid birth certificate bond**, which the bankers fractionally lent, upon manifesting another $9 million dollars out of thin air. This process would then repeat itself to infinity bringing in a minimum of ten million dollars, to hundreds of millions or more, depending on how much money the government thinks you will make over your lifetime.

But there was **one small snag** in all this, in order for the government to write checks from your **pre-paid account**; they have to receive **permission** from you. This occurs when you **voluntarily** sign a social security **SS-5 form**. To **persuade** people to sign this form the government will dangle insurance and retirement **benefits** in your face; but fail to **inform you** of what you are giving up, or rather what you will **become**.

By receiving social security retirement benefits you are now considered to be a **"Federal personnel"***** of the government of the United States, which makes you **ineligible** to challenge the bankruptcy of the United States. And you are no longer considered a **state** citizen but a **14ᵗʰ Amendment citizen**; subjecting you to the **repayment** of the national debt*****.

Accessing and using these funds is beyond the scope of this documentary, however if you like to locate **your prepaid account number** then look for them on either your birth certificate, or within your **IRS individual master file**, or the red colored (cu-sip) **CUSIP serial number** located on the backside of all recently issued **social security cards**.

This will look **different** than your social security number, as it contains **1 letter and 8 numbers**. The first letter designates which one of the **12 Federal Reserve Banks** that is recording **your bond** within its commercial book entry system. And the **8 digit number** is your account number, which is traded as **stock certificate** in either Switzerland or Puerto Rico.

*HJR 192

*On June 5, 1933, congress suspended the gold standard and the gold clause in the national constitution. Since then no one in America has been able to **lawfully** pay a debt.*

*** An **offshore account** which allows **non-resident alien individuals** to obtain tax benefits under foreign law.*

***5 USC 552A (a)(13)

*The term "Federal personnel" means **officers and employees** of the Government of the United States, members of the **uniformed services** (including members of the Reserve Components), individuals entitled to receive immediate or deferred **retirement benefits** under any retirement program of the Government of the United States (including **survivor benefits**).*

****Title code 26 USC 163(h)(3)(B)(ii).

*$1,000,000 limitation: "The aggregate amount treated as **acquisition indebtedness** for any period shall not exceed $1,000,000 ($500,000 in the case of a married individual filing a separate return)."*

*****14th Amendment Section 4.

*The **validity** of the "public debt" of the United States, authorized by law, including debts incurred for payment of* *pensions and bounties for services **in suppressing insurrection or rebellion**, shall not be questioned.*

After the bankruptcy of the corporation of the United States in 1933, its assets were placed under the control of the **Secretary of Treasury*** as its appointed **"receiver"**. And then, in 1944, the corporation's assets were **"quit claimed"** under the control of the newly created **International Monetary Fund**.

The IMF along with the World Bank and GATT were all created, in 1944, during the **Bretton Woods Agreement**. Their polices have allowed the bankers to **capture** within the United States all its gold, national parks, non-profit corporations, all property of **14th amendment citizens**, and even the **birth certificate bonds**.

These assets are now managed by the **Governor of the IMF** who just so happens to be the **Secretary of the Treasury**** and a **paid employee** of the IMF.*** Today the IMF holds a 51% ownership over the corporate government, the IRS, Interpol, and even the **Office of Personnel Management****** which is responsible for sending paychecks to all **federal employees**.

* Reorganization Plan, No. 26, 5 U.S.C.A. 903; Public Law 94-564; Legislative History, pg. 5967.

**(Public Law 94-564, supra, pg. 5942; U.S. Government Manual 1990/91, pgs. 480-81; 26 U.S.C.A. 7701(a)(11); Treasury Delegation Order No. 150-10).

***"The U.S. Secretary of Treasury receives no compensation for representing the United States" — Public Law 94-564, page 8, Section H.R. 13955.

****22 USCA 286f

Not only has the IMF gained **control** over the land and the people of the United States they managed to **steal** all its monetary gold under a system of **institutionalized inflation** created by the Bretton Woods agreement, which dictated that **US tax dollars** would finance the construction of factories in foreign lands to **compete** with American jobs. When this money was being **sent overseas** the United States gold reserve shrank from 80% of the world's gold in 1946, to 22% by 1971. This gold ultimately made its way into the banker's **personal coffers** in mainland Europe.

By the 1960's, **state governors** were becoming concerned of the **IMF takeover** of the American economy and with the legality of **privately issued** Federal Reserve Notes, which had been declared as unlawful money within their own **national and state** constitutions. So in 1962, at the **National Governor's Conference** in Lexington, Kentucky, state governors meet with IMF leaders to discuss solutions to help mitigate the **constitutional crisis** at hand.

They agreed the best approach was to **reincorporate** all states under the same **jurisdiction of the IMF** and to do away with constitutional law, and replacing it with the **tenets** of the **Uniform Commercial Code** and the **Code of Federal Regulations** which can only be enforced in **administrative tribunals** and **admiralty law courts****. This gave them even more control over the people, because instead of the masses **governing themselves** within the limits of the law like the constitution dictates; they would now govern the people under a **strict set of codes** which could be used for corruption. By 1972, all the states had incorporated these **guidelines** and ever since, the people lost all **constitutional** protections.

*****On Oct. 28th 1977, the United States as a "Corporator" and "State" declared insolvency. State banks and most other banks were put under control of the "Governor" of the "Fund" (I.M.F.). — 26 IRC 165 (g)(1); U.C.C. 1-201(23), C.R.S. 39-22-103.5.*

With help from the **Bank of International Settlements**, the **IMF**, and **World Bank**; the international bankers had exported the **American slave grid** to the entire world. In 1945, the **United Nations** organization was established in the heart of the **British colony's financial district** of New York City. Not only had the Crown of England **recaptured her colony** she now had **full control** over the world's financial system.

The corruption of the banks and federal government had become **so pervasive** they truly believed themselves to be above the law. In 1963, **the CIA** murdered John F. Kennedy for **attempting to print** gold and silver backed certificates and for **setting up** a gold backed international reserve currency*.

The Green Hilton Agreement (1963).

President Regan was well aware of what was going on when he was quoted as saying in a **1982 Grace Commission report**, *"None of the federal income tax paid by the American people is ever deposited into the United States Treasury but instead is deposited into the Federal Reserve Bank for its use and benefit!"*

In 1981, Reagan attempted to place the United States on a **gold banking system**. But before he could, he was **assassinated** by John Hinckley, whose family worked closely together in the **oil business** with George Bush Sr.

After his death, Reagan was replaced with a clone** which continued to serve out the presidency **without** the public's knowledge.

***According to Dr. Peter D. Beter, former head of the Export-Import Bank of the United States, Human Cloning first began in 1978.*

Over the passing years, the Federal Reserve System continued to bury the people with debt. The United States was **transformed** from a constitutional republic to a debtor's nation; and then to its **current form** of a legislative democracy **controlled** by a fascist government. And they did so while **transferring** all the assets and future assets of the people **into the hands** of the international bankers.

TO BE CONTINUED IN PART III…(Credit Roll)

Part III
"The Farmer Claims Program"

Since the fall of Atlantis, Satan and his minions have been working tirelessly to end all goodness on this planet. But God and the brotherhood of light had put together their own plan to defeat the dark side. Throughout history many prophets come forth to speak of the coming of a golden age of humanity. This truth was made known only to fall silent on the deaf ears of the ignorant masses. But **change is on the horizon**, the power grab of the elite is coming to an end.

With all their power and money the bankers thought themselves to be **above the law**, but cracks were now appearing in their foundations. Angry Americans were beginning to fight back. A **class action lawsuit** was brewing which would threaten to change the balance of power.

This change began in the mid 1970's, when the **Federal Land Bank** illegally foreclosed on farmers' mortgages all throughout the Midwest. In each of these cases, the farmers were **defrauded** by the banks with the **approval** of the Federal Reserve System. These court cases would eventually become known as the **farmer claims program**.

In 1978 an elderly ranch farmer in Colorado purchased a farm with loan from the **Federal Land Bank**; after he died the property was passed on to his son, **Roy Schwasinger**

Jr., who was a retired military general. Soon after a Federal Land Bank officer and Federal Marshall appeared on his property and informed him that the bank was foreclosing on his farm and to vacate it within 30 days. Without his knowledge, his deceased father had **signed a stipulation** which reverted the property back to the **Federal Land Bank** in the event of the borrower's death.

Outraged, Roy Schwasinger filed a **class action lawsuit** in the Denver Federal Court system. But the case didn't go very far, and the suit was dismissed from filing incorrectly. This began Roy Schwasinger's investigation into the inner workings of the banking system. In 1982, he was given a contract by the **US senate** and later the **Supreme Court** to investigate **banking fraud**. But because he was under a **strict non-disclosure order** he was not allowed to tell the media what he discovered. In the late 80s, he began sharing his knowledge with others, including high ranking military personnel who helped him bring about a **class action lawsuit** against the federal government.

The first series of these lawsuits began in the mid 1980's when William and Shirley Baskerville of Fort Collins, Colorado, were involved in a bankruptcy case with **First Interstate Bank of Fort Collins**; who was trying to foreclose on their farm. At a restaurant their lawyer informed them that he would no longer be able to help them and walked-off. Overhearing the conversation, Roy Schwasinger offered his advice on how to appeal the case in bankruptcy court. So in 1987, they filed **an appeal** (Case No. 87-C-716) with the United States District Court in Colorado.

On November 3, 1988, the Denver Federal Court system ruled that, indeed, the banks had defrauded the

Baskervilles and proceeded to reverse its bankruptcy decision. But when the foreclosed property **was not returned** they filed a **new lawsuit**. Eventually, 23 other farmers, ranchers, and Indians **swindled by the banks in the same manner** would join in the case.

In these cases, the banks were foreclosing on the properties using **fraudulent methods** such as charging exorbitant interest, illegal foreclosure, or by not crediting mortgage payments to their account as they should have, but instead would **steal** the mortgage payments for themselves **triggering foreclosure** on the property. After running out of money they continued their fight without the help of lawyers. With some assistance by the **Farmers Union** a new lawsuit was filed against the Federal Land Bank and the Farmers Credit System. (1)

(1) Case No. 92-C-1781

The District Court ruled in their favor and ordered the banks to **return the stolen properties**; with help from either Federal Marshals or the National Guard. But when no payments were made, the farmers declared **involuntary Chapter Seven Bankruptcy** against the **Federal Land Bank** and the **Farmers Credit System**. The banks appealed their case, insisting that they were not a business but a **federal agency** therefore they were not liable to pay the damages.

So the farmer's legal team adopted a new strategy. According to the **Federal Land Bank's 1933 charter** they are not allowed to make loans directly to applicants, but instead **could only back loans** as a guarantor in case of default. Because the Federal Land Bank had violated this rule the farmer's legal team was able to successfully sue the bank for damages.

Word of the lawsuit began to spread; the legal team would teach others **how to fight foreclosure** and to help them file lawsuits as well (Case No. 93-1308-M). Celebrities such as Willie Nelson joined in the cause and helped raise money during his **"Farm Aid" concerts**. Here is short clip of Willie Nelson describing in his own words the series of events leading up to the farmer claims legal case…

The Baskerville case had now become the **Farmer Claims Class Action Lawsuit**. Worried about the legal ramifications the government retaliated against the farmers by hitting them with either **outrageous IRS fees**, or by imprisoning the legal team under frivolous nonrelated charges. When the farmers realized they were being unfairly targeted, they had **military generals** such as General Roy Schwasinger sit in the courtroom to make sure the bribed judges would vote according to constitutional law.

The farmers, now with a large team of knowledgeable people of the law behind them, filed a new case to claim additional damages from the fraudulent loaning activities of the Farmers Credit System.

The government tried to settle, but they had already lost many cases and were now loosing the appeals as well. More and more evidence was collected. According to the **National Banking Act** all banks are required to register their charters with the **Federal and State Bureau of Records**, but none of the banks had complied, allowing the legal team to sue the Farmers Credit System. Not only was

Farmers Credit System not chartered to do business with the **American Banking Association**, but so were other quasi government organizations such as the Federal Housing Administration, The Department of Housing and Urban Development, and even the Federal Reserve Bank.

The Farmers Claims lawsuit was thrown out of court at each level with the records purposely destroyed. So in the early 1990's, Roy Schwasinger brought the case before the **United States Supreme Court**. Some of the content of this case is sealed from public eyes, but most of it can be viewed today.

Almost unanimously, the U.S. Supreme Court Justices ruled that the **Farmers Union claims** were indeed **VALID**, therefore, all property foreclosed by the Farmers Credit System was illegal and all those who were foreclosed on would have to receive damages. In addition, they ruled that the **U.S. federal government and banks** had defrauded the farmers, and all U.S. citizens, out of vast sums of money and property.

And furthermore, the court ruled the shocking truth that the **IRS was a Puerto Rican Trust and that the Federal Reserve was unlawful**, that the **income tax amendment** was only ratified by four states and therefore **was not a legal amendment**, that the **IRS code was not enacted into "Positive Law"*** within the Code of Federal Regulations, and how the U.S. government illegally foreclosed on farmer's homes with help from federal agencies.

*Positive Law
Laws that have been enacted by a properly instituted and recognized branch of the government.

Irrefutable proof was presented by a retired CIA agent. He provided testimony and records of the banks illegal activities, to plead further evidence that the Farmers' Union claims were indeed legitimate. The implications of such a decision were profound. All gold, silver, and property titles, taken by the Federal Reserve and IRS, must be returned to the people.

The legal team sought assistance from a small group of benevolent visionaries, consisting of politicians, military generals, and business people who have been secretly working to restore the constitution since the mid 1950's. Somehow, within their ranks, a four star U.S. army general received **"title"** and **"receiver"** of the original **1933 United States Bankruptcy**.

When the case was brought before the **U.S. Supreme Court**, they ruled in his favor, giving the Army General **title over the United States, Inc.** Legal action was then passed on to the **Senate Finance Committee** and Senator Sam Nunn, who was working with Roy Schwasinger. With the help of covert congressional and political pressure, President George H.W. Bush issued **an Executive Order**(a) on Oct. 23, 1991, which provided a provision **allowing anyone who has a claim against the federal government to receive payment as long as it's within the rules of the original format of the case**.

(a) Executive Order No. 12778, Principles of Ethical Conduct for Government Officers and Employees; October 23, 1991.

According to the **Federal Reserve Act of 1913**, all present and succeeding debts against the U.S. Treasury must be assumed by the Federal Reserve. Thus the farmer's claims legal team was able to use that executive order to not only force the Federal Reserve to pay out damages in a gold backed currency, but also allow them to receive **legal ownership over the bankruptcy of United States, Inc.**

To collect damages the farmers legal team used an obscure attachment to the 14th amendment which most people are not aware of. **After the civil war the government allowed citizens to claim a payment on anyone who suffered damages as a result of the Federal Government failing to protect its citizens from harm or damages by a foreign government.** President Grant had this attachment sealed from public eyes but somehow, someone the farmer's legal team got a hold of it.

If you listened to that carefully, it specifies **damages by a foreign government**. That foreign government is the **corporate federal government** which has been masquerading to the public as the **constitutional government**. Remember this goes back to the **Organic Act of 1871** and the **Trading with the Enemies Act of 1933**, which defined all citizens as **enemy combatants** under the federal system known as the United States. The Justices and farmer's legal team recognized how evil and corrupt our federal government had become and to counteract this they added some **provisions in the settlement** to bring the government back under control.

   a.   *First they would have to be paid using a lawful currency, backed by gold and silver as the constitution dictates. This would eliminate inflation and gyrating economic cycles created by the Federal Reserve System.*

b. *Second they would be required to* **go back to common** *law instead of admiralty law under the gold fringe flags.* **Under common law if there is no damage or harm done then there is no violation of the law.** *This would eliminate millions of laws which are used to control the masses and protect corrupt politicians.*

c. *Lastly* **the IRS would have to be dismantled** *and replaced with a national sales tax.* **This is the basis of the NESARA Law.**

When the legal team finally settled on a figure, each individual would receive an average of $20 million dollars, payout, per claim. Multiplied by a total of 336,000 claims that were filed against the U.S. Federal Government, the total payout would come out to a staggering $6.6 trillion dollars.

The U.S. Supreme Court placed a **gag order** on the case, struck all information from the Federal Registry, and placed all records in the Supreme Court files. Up to that point Senator Sam Nunn had kept the Baskerville Case records within his office. A settlement was agreed to, out of court, and the decision was sealed by Janet Reno. Because the case was sealed, claimants are not allowed to share court documents to media outlets without violating the settlement, but they can still **tell others about the lawsuit**. This is probably why you have not heard about this.

In 1991, Roy Schwasinger went before a senate committee to present evidence of the banks and governments criminal activity. He informed them how the Corporation of the United States was tied to the establishment of a New World Order which would bring about a **fascist one world government ruled by the international bankers.** So in 1992, a task force was put together consisting of over 300 retired and 35 active US military officers who strongly supported constitutional law.* This task force was responsible for investigating governmental officials, congressional officers, judges, and the Federal Reserve.

  *Chief of Naval Operations, Admiral Jeremy Boorda
  *General David McCloud
  *Former Director of Central Intelligence, William Colby

They uncovered the common practice of **bribery and extortion** committed by both senators and judges. The criminal activity was so rampant that only 2 out of 535 members of congress **were deemed honest.** But more importantly they carried out the **first ever audit** of the Federal Reserve.

The Federal Reserve was used to giving orders to politicians and had no intentions of being audited. However after they were informed their offices would be raided **under military gunpoint** if necessary; they complied with the investigation. After reviewing their files the military officers found $800 trillion dollars sitting in accounts which should have been applied to the national debt. And contrary to federal government propaganda they also discovered that **most nations** had in fact owed money to the United States instead of the other way around.

These hidden trillions were then confiscated and placed into European bank accounts in order to generate the enormous funds needed to pay the farmers claims class action lawsuit, later this money would become the basis of the **prosperity programs**.

Despite these death blows President George H.W. Bush and the illuminati continued on with their plans of global enslavement.

(Listen to NEW world order speech here)

In August 1992, the military officers confronted President Bush and demanded that he sign an agreement that he would return the United States to constitutional law, and ordered him to never use the term New World Order again. Bush *pretended* to cooperate but secretly planned to bring about the New World Order, anyway, by signing an Executive Order on December 25, 1992, that would have indefinitely closed all banks, giving Bush an excuse to declare martial law.

Under the chaos of martial law, Bush intended to install a new constitution which would have kept everyone currently in office in their same position for 25 years, and it would have removed all rights to elect new officials. The military intervened, and stopped Bush from signing that Executive order.

In 1993, members of the Supreme Court, certain members of Congress, and representatives from the Clinton government, meet with high ranking US military officers who were demanding a return to constitutional law, reforms of the banking system, and financial redress. They agreed to create the **farm claims process** which would allow the legal team to set up meetings all over the country on a grass roots level to help others file claims and to educate them about the lawsuit.

A claim of harm could be made on any loan issued by a financial institution for all interest paid; foreclosures; attorney and court fees; IRS taxes or liens; real estate and property taxes; mental and emotional stress caused by the loss of property; stress related illness such as suicide and divorce; and even warrants, incarceration, and probation could also be claimed.

But the Clinton government undermined their efforts by requiring the farm claims **to use a specific form** designed by the government. This form imposed an administrative fee of $300 for each claim, which was later used in 1994 as a basis to arrest the leaders of the legal team, including Roy Schwasinger.

The government was so afraid of what they would say during their trial in Michigan that extra steps were taken to conceal the true nature of the case. County courthouse employees were not allowed to work between Monday and Thursday during the course of the trial. And outside the courthouse, FBI agents swarmed the perimeter preventing the media and visitors from learning what was going on as well.

Harassment and retaliation by the government increased, many were sent to prison, or murdered while incarcerated. Despite being protected by his military personnel, the army general who acquired the original 1933 Title of Bankruptcy of the United States; was imprisoned, killed, and replaced with a clone. This clone was then used as a decoy to prevent any further claims from being filed.

During the first Clinton administration, the military delayed many of Clinton's federal appointments until they were sure these individuals would help restore constitutional law. One such individual who promised to bring about the necessary changes was Attorney General Janet Reno.

In agreement with the Supreme Court ruling on June 3, 1993, Janet Reno ordered the **Delta Force** and **Navy Seals** to Switzerland, England, and Israel, to recapture trillions of dollars of gold stolen by the Federal Reserve System from the strategic gold reserves. These nations cooperated with the raid because they were promised their debts owed to the United States would be canceled and because the people who stole the money from the United States also stole money from their nations as well.

This bullion is to be used for the new currency backed by precious metals. It's now safely stockpiled at the **Norad Complex** at Colorado Springs, Colorado, and four other repositories. Janet Reno's action so enraged the powers-that-be, that it resulted in her death. She was then replaced with a clone, and it was this creature who was responsible for covering-up the various Clinton scandals.

To keep the Secretary of the U.S. Treasury, Robert Rubin, in line, he too was also cloned. For the remainder of their term in office both Reno and Rubin received their salaries from the International Monetary Fund as foreign agents, and not from the U.S. Treasury. Despite these actions the legal team continued on with their fight, while managing to avoid bloodshed and a major revolution.

After 1993 the farmer claims process name was changed to **Bank Claims**. Between 1993 and 1996, the U.S. Supreme Court required U.S. citizens to file **"Bank Claims"** to collect damages paid by the U.S. Treasury Department. This process CLOSED in 1996.

During this time the U.S. Supreme Court assigned one or more Justices **to monitor the progress** of the rulings. They enlisted help of experts in economics, monetary systems, banking, constitutional government and law, and many other related areas. These justices built coalitions of support and assistance with thousands of people worldwide; **known as 'White Knights"**. The term 'White Knights' was borrowed from the world of big business. It refers to a vulnerable company that is rescued by a corporation, or a wealthy person, from a hostile takeover.

To implement the required changes, the five Justices **spent years** negotiating how the reformations would occur. Eventually they settled on certain agreements, also known as **'Accords'** with the U.S. government, the Federal Reserve Bank owners, the International Monetary Fund, the World Bank, and with numerous other countries, including the United Kingdom and countries of the Euro Zone. Because these U.S. banking reformations **will impact the entire world**; the IMF, World Bank, and other countries had to be involved. **The reformations require that the Federal Reserve be absorbed by the U.S. Treasury Department and the banks' fraudulent activities must be stopped and payment must be made for past harm.**

In 1998, the military generals who originally participated in the famer's claim process realized that the US Supreme Court justices had no intentions of implementing the 'Accords'. So they decided **the only way to implement the reformations** was through a law passed by congress. In 1999, a **75 page document** known as the **National Economic Security and Reformation Act** (NESARA) was submitted to Congress where it sat with little action for almost a year.

Late one evening, on March 9, 2000, a written quorum call was hand-delivered by **Delta Force and Navy SEALS** to 15 members of the US Senate and the US House who were sponsors and co-sponsors of NESARA. They were immediately escorted by the **Delta Force and Navy SEALS** to their respective voting chambers where they passed the **National Economic Security and Reformation Act**.

These 15 members of congress were the **only people lawfully allowed to hold office** in accordance with the original 13th amendment. Remember British soldiers destroyed copies of the **Titles of Nobility Amendment** (TONA) in the war of 1812, because it prevented anyone who had ties to the Crown of England from holding public office.

NESARA is the most ground breaking reformation to sweep not only this country, but our planet, in its entire history. The act does away with the Federal Reserve Bank, the IRS, the shadow government, and much more.

NESARA implements the following changes:

1. Zeros out all credit card, mortgage, and other bank debt due to illegal banking and government activities. This is the Federal Reserve's worst nightmare, a "jubilee" or a forgiveness of debt.

2. Abolishes the income tax

3. Abolishes the IRS. Employees of the IRS will be transferred into the US Treasury national sales tax area.

4.   Creates a 14% flat rate non-essential 'new items only' sales tax revenue for the government. In other words food and medicine will not be taxed; nor will used items such as old homes.

5.   Increases benefits to senior citizens

6.   Returns Constitutional Law to all courts and legal matters.

7.   Reinstates the original Title of Nobility Amendment. Hundreds of thousands of Americans under the control of foreign powers will lose their citizenship, be deported to other countries, and barred from reentry for the remainder of their life. And millions of people will soon discover their college degrees are now worthless paper.

8.   Establishes new Presidential and Congressional elections within 120 days after NESARA's announcement. The intern government will cancel all "National Emergencies" and return us back to constitutional law.

9.   Monitors elections and prevents illegal election activities of special interest groups.

10.   Creates a new U.S. Treasury, 'rainbow currency,' backed by gold, silver, and platinum precious metals, ending the bankruptcy of the United States initiated by Franklin Roosevelt in 1933.

11.   Forbids the sale of American birth certificate records as chattel property bonds by the US Department of Transportation.

12.   Initiates new U.S. Treasury Bank System in alignment with Constitutional Law

13. Eliminates the Federal Reserve System. During the transition period the Federal Reserve will be allowed to operate side by side of the U.S. treasury for one year in order to remove all Federal Reserve notes from the money supply.

14. Restores financial privacy

15. Retrains all judges and attorneys in Constitutional Law

16. Ceases all aggressive, U.S. government military actions worldwide

17. Establishes peace throughout the world

18. Releases enormous sums of money for humanitarian purposes

19. Enables the release of over 6,000 patents of suppressed technologies that are being withheld from the public under the guise of national security, including free energy devices, antigravity, and sonic healing machines.

(Listen to and watch Clip of Clinton)

Because President Clinton's clone had no interest in signing NESARA into law, on October 10, 2000; under orders from U.S. military generals the elite **Naval Seals and Delta Force** stormed the White House and under gunpoint forced Bill Clinton to sign NESARA. During this time **Secret Service** and **White House security personnel** were ordered to stand down, disarmed, and allowed to witness this event under a gag order.

From its very inception Bush Sr., the corporate government, major bank houses, and the Carlyle group have opposed NESARA. To maintain secrecy, the case details and the docket number were sealed and revised within the official congressional registry, to reflect a commemorative coin, and then again it was revised even more recently. This is why there are no public **Congressional Records** and why a search for this law will not yield the correct details until after the reformations are made public.

You probably never heard of this law due to an extremely strict gag order placed upon politicians, media personnel, and bank officers. Even though Alex Jones or Ron Paul will not tell you about it, the law is still valid.

And members of Congress will not tell us any of this because they have been ordered by the U.S. Supreme Court Justices to **'deny' the existence of NESARA** or face charges of treason punishable by death. Some members of Congress have actually been charged with **'obstruction.'** Minnesota Senator Paul Wellstone was about to break the gag order, but before he could, his small passenger plane crashed killing his wife, daughter, and himself.

If fear isn't enough to keep Congress in line, money is. The CIA routinely bribes Senators with stolen loot from the bank roll programs. Every Senator has been bribed with a minimum of $200 million dollars deposited in a **Bank of America** account in Canada. You will never hear the media networks report about NESARA. To maintain silence, major news networks, such as CNN, are paid to the tune of $2 billion dollars annually. Some of this loot is funneled by the **Mormon Church in Utah**, through Senator Orin Hatch's office and Bank of America.

Not only is Congress bribed, but the entire Joint Chiefs of Staff, and upper tier of the government, including the president, receives these payments as well. Only the **Provost Marshall** has the lawful authority to arrest these individuals, but sadly he won't do his job either. It seems the United State military is full of **pencil pushing politicians** who care more about advancement then doing their job.

And not surprisingly, much **disinformation** about NESARA can be found on the Internet. Prominent nay-sayers include quatloos.com, which is rumored to be a CIA front; nesara.org which is maintained by the Bush family; Sherry Shriner; and various Internet channelers receiving their messages from telepathic spooks, have all contributed to the confusion.

Even the information on Wikipedia is in error. Wikipedia gives you the history of CIA agent Harvey Barnard's NESARA law. If you look closely, this law stands for **National Economic Stabilization and Recovery Act**, which would have made reforms to the economy and replace the income tax with a national sales tax. This law was rejected by Congress in the 1990's. But there is little mention of the **National Economic Security and Reformation Act** on Wikipedia or its ramifications.

September 11, 2001

The next step is to announce NESARA to the world, but it's not an easy task to do. Many powerful groups have tried to prevent the implementation of NESARA.

The NESARA law requires that at least once a year, an effort be made to announce the law to the public. Three current US Supreme Court judges control the committee in charge of NESARA's announcement. These Judges have used their overall authority to secretly sabotage NESARA's announcement.

In 2001, after much negotiation, the Supreme Court justices ordered the current Congress to pass resolutions 'approving' NESARA. This took place on September 9, 2001, eighteen months after NESARA became law. On September 10, 2001, George Bush Sr. moved into the White house to steer his son on how to block the announcement. The next day, on September 11, 2001, at 10 am Eastern Daylight Time, Alan Greenspan was scheduled to announce the **new US Treasury Bank system, debt forgiveness for all U.S. citizens, and abolishment of the IRS**, as the first part of the public announcements of NESARA.

Just before the announcement, at 9 am, Bush Sr. ordered the demolition of the **World Trade Center** to stop the international banking computers on floors one and two, in the North Tower from initiating the **new U.S. Treasury Bank system**. Explosives in the World Trade Center were planted by both CIA and Mossad operatives, and detonated remotely, in Building 7, which was demolished later that day, in order to cover-up their crime.

Remote pilot technology was used in a flyover event to deliver a payload of explosives into the Pentagon at the exact location of the **White Knights** in their new **Naval Command Center**, who were coordinating activities supporting NESARA's implementation nationwide. With the announcement of NESARA stopped dead in its tracks, George Bush Sr. decapitated any hopes of returning the government back to the people.

While CIA agent, Osama Bin Laden, is made into the boogeyman, the country dashed off to fight a **"war on terror"**. The events of 9/11 eventually led the way to the slaughter of the Iraqi people. To keep the public unaware of the carnage, **the official death count** of US soliders and Iraqi civilians is purposely underreported. Deceased US soldiers are either being dumped into the Persian Gulf or replaced with clones. As of 2009, the total death count of Iraqi civilians now surpasses a staggering 1.6 million people.

The same cooked statistics apply to the death totals on the day of 9/11. According to the government, 2,752 people died that day. When in actuality, 30,700 people had died. No one questions the insanely small numbers given out by the government, because New York City is a large place; people who have lost loved ones do not make contact with other survivors, so they have no way of knowing how many have truly died.

(SILENT BLACK SCREEN FLASHING THESE STATS - use sobering piano music)

"WAR ON TERROR" CASUALTIES REPORT
Operation Iraqi Freedom Actual Statistics
March 20, 2003 to January 26, 2007

U.S. soldiers killed in Iraq
    50,500
U.S. soldiers, war injuries
    22,800
U.S. civilians killed
    5,000

U.S. soldier bodies dumped into Persian Gulf
   7,000
Iraqis soldiers killed
   81,000
Iraqis civilians killed
   1,650,000
Iraqis injured
   555,000

Operation Iraqi Freedom Official Statistics
According to the United States Department of
Defense

Confirmed U.S. soldiers dead
   3,896
U.S soldier, hostile injuries
   28,661

Operation Enduring Freedom
Afghanistan War Actual Statistics
October 7, 2001 to December 25, 2007

U.S. soldiers killed
   12,000
U.S. soldiers, war injuries
   N/A
Afghans soldiers killed
   35,000
Afghans civilians killed
   30,500
Afghans injuries
   67,400

Operation Enduring Freedom
Afghanistan War Official Statistics According to the United States Department of Defense.

U.S. soldiers official deaths
   746
First Gulf War
January 16, 1991 till April 6, 1991

U.S. soldiers killed in Iraq
   24,000
U.S. Veterans who died since 1991 from causes of the war
   22,000
Iraq soldiers killed
   56,000
Iraq civilians killed
   43,000
Iraq civilians killed since the war - January 1991 till March 2003 — 405,000

Clones used to replace killed U.S. Soldiers
Not reported in all three wars
   72,000

9/11 - World Trade Tower Disaster

Total deaths to date resulting from this disaster
   56,600
Actual number of people killed that day
   30,700

Number of the 30,700 picked up by Starship that day
20,400
Official death toll
2,752
Officially identified
1,527

Banking Packets

The Bush family was originally offered $300 trillion dollars to cooperate with NESARA, but instead they choose to maintain their control over us, so in the end the Bush family will end up with nothing. The attacks of 9/11 had managed to stop the announcement of NESARA dead in its tracks. Many more attempts have been made over the years but the bush family has managed to stop them. These people won't be able to get away with their crimes forever; little by little their wealth is being dismantled right before their eyes.

Before NESARA is announced to the public it was stipulated that the original farmer claims must be paid out with a bullion backed currency issued by the U.S. Treasury system. In other words, they cannot be paid in Federal Reserve Notes. The $6.6 trillion dollar farmer claims payout is to be distributed in the form of ATM debit cards. Remember this money will come from the bank roll and prosperity programs. The only catch is, to distribute these funds they must first be released by the trustees whose members come from the Clinton, Bush, and Rockefeller families.

They are doing everything they possibly can to stop these payouts. One way is to transport the banking documents, which contain instructions on how to access these funds, in a never-ending loop 24/7 between warehouses in Charlotte, NC and Washington D.C. The drivers of these Fed Ex trucks are heavily bribed and many of them are afraid of being arrested by the Department Homeland Security if they were to actually deliver their payload as required by law. At one point, after the packets were returned to Washington D.C., President George W. Bush placed them under military guard. Federal judges ordered him to release the funds but Bush replied. "You will never receive these packages, they belong to me." The judge answered, "I can do no more; he is the President of the United States." The only option left is to arrest the president, but the Police Commissioner, Provost Marshal, and the Military refuse to help.

This cycle has been on-going for years; the only alternative left is to kill the Federal Reserve System by force. The problem is President George Bush and now Obama has threatened to use the dollar as a weapon of mass destruction against the nations of the world to comply with the New World Order agenda. Bush once commented, "The people will now suffer greatly."

The world cannot tolerate this; the dollar must be removed as an International Reserve Currency and replaced with a new independent asset-based monetary unit backed by precious metals.

On December 15, 2006, a meeting was arranged to discuss ways to curtail these criminal activities. Their ranks included representatives from the Global Family, who are enlightened individuals working directly under Saint Germain. They include members from the IMF; World Bank, Rothschild family, and key persons from over 48 nations.

They agreed to implement three goals by June 15, 2007, that is....

1. To end all war.
2. To actively improve the environment.
3. To actively provide abundance for their people.

Those nations which did not keep this agreement would eventually be cut off from the international banking community in order to force them into compliance. On September 19, 2007, a new gold back banking system was approved by Congress. On October 19, 2007, at midnight, the U.S. treasury of the Republic went on-line with the new global banking system. But this gold banking system is not being deployed because the banks are trying to dispose of their worthless derivatives before they get reset to zero when the gold backed currency valuations go into force.

To improve the stability of the banking system, in 1988, the **Bank of International Settlements** implemented **Basel I** which required banks to hold 6% net capital*. On December 1, 2007, this went a step further when **Basel II** was implemented requiring all loans to be backed by the appropriate collateral, and raised net capital requirements to 8%. The new rules prevent the bankers from collateralizing their derivatives with stolen money from the collateral accounts and prosperity funds. Furthermore, all assets must be valued according to the **daily market price** also known as the **"mark to market" rule**. Any bank which refuses to comply with Basel II will be **cut off from international markets**, which is why American banks demanded $700 billion dollars from the **Trouble Assets Relief Program**;

if they didn't get this bailout, the banks would have shut their doors, inciting martial law.

  * A firm's net worth, minus deductions for any asset that is not easily converted into cash at their full value.

On June 15, 2009, **Basel III** was initiated which goes a step further than **Basel II** by requiring the banks to disclose any previously undisclosed "junk asset" or derivative parked off the balance sheet. Jack Blum has investigated financial fraud for the federal government for over 30 years; he has found that the banks use **off-balance sheet financial operations** to hide money in places like the Cayman Islands.

  (Grab a clip from tax havens and the hidden hand 2:30-2:50)

Under **Basel III** every bank transaction must be disclosed on the balance sheet, but if this was to happen these banks will become insolvent overnight and would not be able to pass their fake "Stress Test". The Federal Reserve System is fighting tooth and nail to prevent this disclosure, because if their $500 trillion dollars or so of derivatives were actually placed on their balance sheet, using the mark to market rule, they will be shown to be bankrupt.

Some banks are now working to bring about the NESARA mission in the hopes that some of the prosperity funds would trickle into their banks saving them from closing their doors. **But most of the larger banks that are fighting the coming changes will soon be out of business.** They are not informing their employees of the new regulations and thus will not be ready to operate under a gold banking charter.

Slowly the illegal practices of the international financiers are coming to an end. One-by-one, the major banking houses are imploding right before our eyes. Their train wreck is occurring because these banks are no longer allowed to use assets from the **Collateral Accounts** of the **Global Debt Facility** to back up their loans.

This is why we are seeing the derivatives implode. The banks have been illegally using the **collateral accounts** as collateral for their gold backed derivatives, bullion certificates, and bonds sold through offshore domiciled corporations. With the **new Basel II rules** in place, these paper assets have now become worthless garbage, resulting in the massive **banking "write-downs"** you see today. According to **Office of International Treasury Control** this over the counter derivative market is worth about $3.3 quadrillion dollars, with J.P. Morgan leading the pack with hundreds of trillions of dollars of derivatives.

During the Clinton years, the banking **1:10 fractional reserve ratio** was increased to **1:100**. This easy money allowed anyone to get a home loan resulting in the **housing sector boom.** Since many of these loans were made to risky low income households, the banks deferred their risk by selling their **loan portfolios** to investors in a process known as **securitization.** This occurs when mortgages are repackaged with other mortgages, into a giant pool of liquidity, which are sold to investors on the global market. These **credit derivatives** can then be repackaged and leveraged again at *another* **1:100 ratio**, which can be repeated over and over; until there is literally **quadrillions of dollars of derivatives** floating around in the worlds banking system. When housing prices were going up these derivatives were making fortunes for the banks and governments offshore accounts; allowing them to buy up assets all over the world with virtually free money. When investors realized these derivatives contained toxic loans, they stop their buying binge, causing the credit market to seize up, which is why housing prices are in freefall.

Because no one wants to buy these toxic derivatives, the banks and the government are now in a panic to find **other people's money** to plug up the holes in their cracking dam. Though some funds have been raised by either **selling military secrets to China** or through **CIA drug running operations**, this is nowhere near enough money to prop up a collapsing derivative market. So now the government is resorting to **stealing the money** which is no credible way to run a country. To put a stop this criminal activity, in December 2009, Interpol was given legal jurisdiction within the US to hunt down and arrest corrupt bankers.

April 4th 2008, marked the expiration of the 70 year bankruptcy agreement of the United States, beginning in 1938. Technically, the bankruptcy began in 1933, but the Supreme Court did not enforce it until the United States became a **"legislative democracy"** in 1938*.

*ERIE R.R. vs Thompkins

The nations of the world, weary of the chancery of the Federal Reserve System, knew they had a limited time to foreclose on the United States, before the corporate government could extend another 70 year extension of the bankruptcy. Without this protection the government was now at the mercy of its creditors, who were demanding reforms of the banking system, such as higher net capital requirements found under **Basel II**. If the United States failed to meet their demands, they would be cut off from international markets.

So to raise the funds needed in August 2008, the U.S. government began shorting the derivative market, causing stock and commodity prices to fall worldwide. But this $20 trillion dollars of wealth was not destroyed, but instead it was transferred into the government's offshore pension fund accounts. Of which $5 trillion dollars was moved back into the United States to shore up a collapsing dollar. Soon this money will run out, leaving the option of either crashing the financial markets once again; destroying what little is left of the American economy, or by printing more money leading to hyperinflation.

But the global family does not want to see a devalued dollar, as 90% of all U.S. dollars in circulation today are held by foreigners, and they have no desire to see their assets evaporate. So they have agreed to back all dollars printed before September 2008, with gold stored in the Philippines, at a rate of 1/28th of a gram of gold per dollar. This will serve to curb the inflationary activities of the Federal Reserve and the assets of the hard working average American. But on the other hand, all derivatives will be valued at 1/3 of 1% percent, which is their fair market value, forcing those who own this toxic trash into bankruptcy and finally out of business.

On September 30, 2009, the fiscal year of the United States came to a close. Because of the precarious financial situation of the United States and its derivative holdings the Chinese government reversed its policy of accepting fiat money for repayment of the national debt. Instead they will only accept gold and silver as lawful payment, as specified in Article 1 Section 10 of the United States Constitution*. To meet these new demands, the owners of the Federal Reserve System are scrambling to purchase enough gold and silver, but no one wants to sell them any.

*Section 10. ...make any Thing but gold and silver Coin a Tender in Payment of Debts.

While the Federal Reserve System is falling apart, Barry Soetoro continues to block the NESARA deliveries. Even though he never invested any money in these programs he demands a portion of these funds for himself. In a pattern which mimics the Bush years, the Obama administration continues makes numerous daily attempts to steal the funds.

Before he was even sworn in office, in December 2008, Obama tried unsuccessfully to steal $400 billion from the prosperity funds, and demanded another $1 trillion ransom for his deed. A week before his inauguration, Saint Germain and the global family had confronted Obama about his actions. At that time Obama agreed to go along with the NESARA mission, but soon after reversed his promise and has now solidified his alliance with the Bush/Clinton cabal.

In March 2009, Obama tried once again to steal over $200 trillion dollars of international funds from the Bank of International Settlements. This money was originally stolen by the Nazi's from holocaust victims, and for the past 60 years has been earning interest in secret bank accounts. When Obama was informed that **theft of international funds is an impeachable offense** he replied, "You can't touch me, I'm above it, we knew where it was, so we took it".

As the largest holder of the national debt, the Chinese government is now in control of the United States economy, its grain supply, and its communist President; which is why Chinese President Hu does not want to see NESARA announced, otherwise it would negate this cushy arrangement. In May 2009, Obama sought help from the Chinese government to hack into some the trust accounts overseas. Had Obama been successful, China would have received a $4 trillion dollar payout for their cooperation. Thankfully, the white knights located the money, and it is now in a safe place.

So, who was really benefiting from a Chicago Olympics?

In anticipation of the proposed Chicago Olympics site, Obama had committed to buy several hundred million dollars of property in the surrounding area with borrowed money from the US Treasury. He then promised to pay a huge bribe to **International Olympic Committee** using stolen money from the prosperity funds. When he arrived empty handed, after failing to access the accounts, they immediately threw Chicago out of the running and now Obama is stuck with a bunch of worthless slum land and a huge debt to the US Treasury.

In another incident, Obama demanded 58% of the program money to be paid to him into his personal bank account, with the rest of the money to be taxed at a rate of 65%. Both the Queen of England, President of France Nicolas Sarkozy, and German Chancellor Angela Merkel, agreed to these terms, and why not, after all, it's not their money they are giving away.

The Queen of England has also participated in this sabotage; she has placed **secret override codes** into these banking computers which allow her ladyship and Obama to move this money around and around until "hell freezes over." Awaiting the time until they can figure out how to access these funds.

To garner the cooperation of Bush Senior and Obama, the global family offered to pay 0.5% for all their fraudulent derivatives and warehouses of stolen loot in exchange for the new gold back US treasury currency. This offer was turned down, and a new offer was made at 2.5%, with Obama getting 2.5% of that. Even though these percentages may appear to be small they are based on quadrillions of dollars, so we are talking enormous amounts of money. This offer was also refused, and now they are demanding a 100% exchange, along with an agreement to escape exposure and prosecution. This offer was flatly turned down.

To pay for the **United States Healthcare Bill**, Obama attempted to raise $44.5 trillion through the sale of a **Health Care Revenue Anticipation Bond** in Switzerland, with a 35 year term collateralized by the **Freedom bank roll program**; of this, $42 trillion was to go to Obama personally, and the other $2.5 trillion will pay for the government's takeover of healthcare. The only problem is that Obama had the signatures forged along with a few senior democratic senators and congressmen, who are now demanding his impeachment. When Swiss authorities realized the signatures where forged, they proceeded to turn over the evidence to the **International Court of Justice**. Obama tried to block this action through an executive order, but no one seems to be paying it much attention.

The reason Obama wanted $42 trillion dollars is because he has been borrowing money heavily from the banks* in order to bribe anyone who dares to oppose him. These loans are collateralized using forged signatures of prosperity program receipts, and their corresponding bank trades. This loaned money is then used to bribe **world court judges** to look the other way. But because the White Knights are blocking these transactions, Obama is going deeper and deeper into debt. The banks are starting to realize that a trap being set for them, but sadly it's too late, there is no way they can recover from these mega-loan losses. They may think they can simply destroy evidence of these transactions and hope that the problem goes away, but luckily duplicates can be found through state auditors.

*Bank of America, Citibank, Goldman Sachs, JPMorgan Chase, and Wachovia.

When Obama is confronted with these criminal actions his typical response is, *"As long as I am President, which will be for another 12 or 18 years or whatever I decide because I am the RULER, you will never get this money and eventually I will get all of it one way or another."* When referring to the American people Obama was quoted as saying. *"They are scum and trash and they do not need or deserve this money".*

One source has even quoted him as saying *"I am KING, I am GOD".* Obama's arrogance may stem from the plans of George Bush Senior and the Thule Society to crown Obama as a **God king** under a 1,000 year Reich beginning in 2012.

For these reasons the White Knights have ordered Obama to submit his resignation papers if he wishes to avoid treason. But Obama simply laughs it off and replies *"You can't charge me, besides, the House and the Senate will never go along with it because they are just as guilty as I am"*. He then continues to insist that the funds are his to do as he pleases as he is "the ruler of this country".

The longer Obama remains in office, the closer America teeters on economic collapse. Personal income tax collections are down 40%, and for corporations, 67%. Housing values have dropped 80% in some areas. Farmers are having a hard time getting a loan to plant new crops, which means many innocent people could pay with their lives.

While the United States economy implodes, the government continues to borrow trillions of dollars to fund pet projects and bailout failed business models such as GM and Chrysler. The government debts generated from these bailouts are flooding the bond market making it even harder for the private sector to get a loan to survive. These actions are also **hyperinflationary** which will ultimately lead to a collapsing dollar and higher prices for Americans.

The banks, now fresh with slush money from their bailouts and bonuses, could care less if the economy comes crashing down. In December 2008, access to credit card lines was reduced from $5 trillion to $3 trillion dollars. Sadly, this lifeline is being cut off from the American people at a time when they are losing their jobs.

In preparation for economic collapse, and the New World Order, Obama has now increased preparedness for martial law, which under **Rex84** would send millions of patriotic Americans to concentrations camps. Should this occur the White Knights are prepared to take strong actions to protect the American people. Whether the NESARA transition is peaceful or not, God has mandated that the common man will not suffer. The dark side's plans for massed vaccinations, martial law, or nuclear war, will end in utter failure, and those who cooperated with such schemes will descend into the ash heap of history.

The peoples of the world are now becoming aware of these grievances. Queen Elizabeth and the Crown of England have both gone too far with their crown power. Third world nations, such as Malaysia, will no longer allow the **International Monetary Fund** to rape their assets. African and South American nations, once devastated by the IMF, are now teaming up to create their own coalitions. Attempts by the international banking community to crush the Islamic nations have yielded little results; as they continue to abide to the gold standard, as dictated in the Koran. China is proposing the creation of new **international reserve currency** backed by precious metals which would operate outside the manipulations of the **Bank of International Settlements** and the **Committee of 300***.

*The **Committee of 300** is an offshoot of the British East India Company's **Council of 300** founded by British aristocracy in 1727. Their goals include globalism, depopulation, and a one world government.*

In addition to the financial reforms, **the Vatican has agreed to cooperate** with a plan to end poverty and turn the deserts green, by allowing the development of **forbidden technologies** such as free energy. The White Hats in the

US Space Command, which operate bases like Area 51, are now ready to release **antigravity and teleportation technologies** which would make all automobiles and airplanes obsolete. Industries which are expected to vanish completely, include petroleum, war, nuclear power, pharmaceuticals, and automobiles. Companies in these industries will receive substantial financial help after NESARA, in order to transform themselves for the coming changes. For example, the petroleum industry could be turned into a **geo-engineering industry**, the armaments industry could move into **space exploration**, and car manufacturers could be retooled to produce **antigravity scooters**.

The longer these bankers and the corporate federal government refuse to go along with NESARA; the more **banking implosions** we will see. The world has announced, **enough is enough**, if you do not behave yourselves you will be shut off from the international community.

Nearly three hundred years have passed; since the creation of Saint Germain's **"World Trust"**. The time has now come to herald in a **new age of peace and prosperity**. We do not want an economic collapse, martial law, or a New World Order; **we want NESARA NOW!**

Special Thanks To:

The Francis Bacon Society
Peter Dawkins
Teamlaw.org
Walter Burien
CAFR1.com
Patrick Bellringer

Fourwinds10.com
The Casper Updates
The Benjamin Fulford Reports
Office of International Treasury Control
The Dove Reports
Nesara.us
General Roy Schaswinger
Admiral Jeremy Michael Boorda
The White Knights
The Farmer Claims Legal Team

SUPREME PRODUCTIONS

CHANGE IS ON THE HORIZON
Written by James Rink.

James Rink, researcher, author, and film producer.

He has produced **"Change is on the Horizon"** which is a three hour video documentary delving into banking, finance, constitutional law and **NESARA: the National Economic Security and Reformation Act.**

He has helped to awaken humanity to the secret activities of the covert government, covering topics such brainwashing, trauma, milabs (which stands for military abductions, and covert harassment, both of which he has had to endure for his entire life, as a product of Project Surrogate and Ultra MK Milab experimentations).

His book **"Lone Wolf"** chronicles these projects.

He now spends his time perfecting the **"Neo Meditation Cube"** — a chi energizer that helps users relax during meditation so that they can integrate themselves.

Thanks to the Neo, James has been able to work around the programming and trauma he has been forced to endure.

Dawn of the Golden Age   123

Other Publications
by David E. Robinson

Dawn of the Golden Age 125

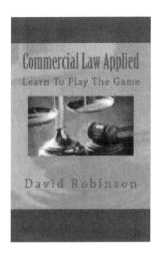

Commercial Law Applied

Learn To Play The Game
Authored by David E. Robinson

The principles, maxims and precepts of Commercial Law are eternal, unchanging and unchangeable. They are expressed in the Bible, both in the Old Testament and in the New.

The law of commerce — unchanged for thousands of years — forms the underlying foundation of all law on this planet; and for governments around the world. It is the law of nations, and of everything that human civilization is built upon.

This is why Commercial Law is so powerful.

When you operate at the level of Commercial Law, by these precepts, nothing that is of inferior statute can overturn or change it, or abrogate it, or meddle with it. It is the fundamental source of all authority, power and functional reality.

https://www.createspace.com/3960715

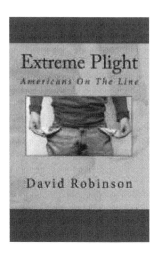

Extreme Plight

Americans On The Line

Authored by David E. Robinson

The 545 People Responsible for all of America's Woes.

Politicians are the only people in the world who create problems and then campaign against them.

Have you ever wondered why, if both the Democrats and the Republicans are against deficits, we have deficits? Have you ever wondered why, if all the politicians are against inflation and high taxes, we have inflation and high taxes?

You and I don't propose a federal budget. The president does. You and I don't have the Constitutional authority to vote on appropriations. The House of Representatives does. You and I don't write the tax code. Congress does. You and I don't set fiscal policy. Congress does. You and I don't control monetary policy. The Federal Reserve Bank does.

One hundred senators, 435 congressmen, one president and nine Supreme Court justices - 545 human beings out of the 235 million - are directly, legally, morally and individually responsible for the domestic problems that plague this country.

https://www.createspace.com/4021130

19. **Monitions of a Mountain Man**
    https://www.createspace.com/3398756
20. **Hope Deferred**
    https://www.createspace.com/3761587
21. **History of World Banking**
    https://www.createspace.com/3715660
22. **Gun Carry In The USA**
    https://www.createspace.com/3610190
23. **Maine Republic Email Alerts**
    https://www.createspace.com/3845798
24. **Manual for the united States...**
    https://www.createspace.com/3556384
25. **Forming Jural Assemblies**
    https://www.createspace.com/3563660
26. **Policies, Procedures & Protocols**
    https://www.createspace.com/3576921
27. **The Palin Road Ahead**
    https://www.createspace.com/3530763
28. **Climategate Debunked**
    https://www.createspace.com/3432946
29. **The Bible As Reform**
    https://www.createspace.com/3475724
30. **The Bible As History**
    https://www.createspace.com/3475727
31. **The Bible As Healing**
    https://www.createspace.com/3475725
32. **Deceived**
    https://www.createspace.com/3406527
33. **Mary Baker Eddy Disobeyed**
    https://www.createspace.com/3436591
34. **Mary Baker Eddy Betrayed**
    https://www.createspace.com/3488684
35. **Mary Baker Eddy Betrayed**
    https://www.createspace.com/3488688
36. **Mary Baker Eddy Betrayed**
    https://www.createspace.com/3488696

1. Nesara I
   https://www.createspace.com/3676730
2. Nesara II
   https://www.createspace.com/3694967
3. Be The One
   https://www.createspace.com/3921716
4. Commercial Redemption
   https://www.createspace.com/3397150
5. Hardcore Redemption-in-Law
   https://www.createspace.com/3475497
6. Commercial Law Applied
   https://www.createspace.com/3960715
7. The Matrix As It Is
   https://www.createspace.com/3495158
8. Give Yourself Credit
   https://www.createspace.com/3462990
9. From Debt To Prosperity
   https://www.createspace.com/3485734
10. DebtOcracy
    https://www.createspace.com/3650756
11. Asset Protection
    https://www.createspace.com/3700522
12. Untold History Of America
    https://www.createspace.com/3407070
13. New Beginning Study Course
    https://www.createspace.com/3412422
14. Reclaim Your Sovereignty
    https://www.createspace.com/3418256
15. Oil Beneath Our Feet
    https://www.createspace.com/3420496
16. The People's Voice
    https://www.createspace.com/3724222
17. My Home Is My Castle
    https://www.createspace.com/3464566
18. Maine Street Miracle
    https://www.createspace.com/3397262

Made in the USA
Columbia, SC
01 December 2020